MAY 2002

941.0859 LEWA
Lewandowski,
A Yank in the
/

WITHDRAWN

A YANK IN THE VILLAGE

A YANK IN THE VILLAGE

Thoughts about life in and out of England from a former Brooklyn girl who once wished she was Jane Eyre

Linda Lewandowski

The Book Guild Ltd
Sussex, England

First published in Great Britain in 2001 by
The Book Guild Ltd
25 High Street
Lewes, East Sussex
BN7 2LU

Copyright © Linda Lewandowski 2001

The right of Linda Lewandowski to be identified as the author of this work has been asserted by her in accordance with the Copyright, Designs and Patents Act 1988.

All rights reserved. No part of this publication may be reproduced, transmitted, or stored in a retrieval system, in any form, or by any means, without permission in writing from the publishers, nor be otherwise circulated in any form of binding or cover other than that in which it is published and without a similar condition being imposed on the subsequent purchaser.

Typesetting in Times by
SetSystems Ltd, Saffron Walden, Essex

Printed in Great Britain by
Bookcraft (Bath) Ltd, Avon

A catalogue record for this book is
available from the British Library

ISBN 1 85776 568 0

*For the Villagers of
Potterspury
Yardley Gobion
Cosgrove
&
Paulerspury*

Contents

New Girl in Town	1
My Friends at Currys	3
The Return of the Fly	6
Bits and Pieces	9
Behind the Wheel	12
The Unlikely Ambassador	15
Ameri-Speak Quiz	18
Down on the Farm	21
Bumper Stickers	25
Do I Miss the USA?	27
The REAL Superstore	31
The 24-Hour Office	34
Yuletide Bits and Pieces	37
School	40
Time for a Whinge	44
Reflections on Expatriation	47
Parenthood	51
Hanging Up the Laundry	56
About Cake and Coffee	59
Salad Bar None	63
Traffic School	67

A Yank En Route to LA	70
To Market! To Market!	74
Food for Thought	77
My Top 25 Reasons for Wanting to Stay Here Forever (at least for now)	81
L.S.M.F.T.	85
Transatlantic Confusion	90
Clinton's Calamity	95
Doing Business in the UK	99
My Life as a Storyteller	103
Volunteering	108
Am I Blushing?	114
Welcome to the United States	118
A Story	122
Good Ol' Mare	126
Due to current political, economic and social constraints, the light at the end of the tunnel has been turned off until further notice.	130
... American Style	134
How I Spent My Summer Vacation	138
Overexposed	143
Loo Habits	147
Internet Humour	150
At War with My Major and Minor Appliances	154
'You'll Go Bald, You Know!'	158
The Yank is Going Back	163
To Be a Hero	167
The Final Hours	171
Really Back in the USA	177

Acknowledgements

The day after I arrived in England, a man on bicycle approached my back door to present me with my mail. This was a pivotal moment for me for two reasons. While my children and I had enjoyed reading about postmen on bicycles, we had never actually seen the real thing in suburban America. Having my very own jolly postman smile at me, hand me my mail and pedal off confirmed I really was in England.

He also handed me my copy of the free monthly newsletter that served three villages in what I would eventually come to see as my 'neighbourhood'. As I sat down to read *The Old Mail*, I came upon the odd poem or two among the local news items. The casual writer in me beckoned.

I could write something for this newsletter. Why don't I write a monthly column about an American's view of life in the English countryside? Very tongue-in-cheek, of course. Why, I'll call it A Yank in the Village*!*

Bubbling with enthusiasm, and never having heard of Bill Bryson, I called my village editor, Mags Fenn, and gushed out my plan. 'You don't know me, but . . .' I began. Cautious, yet courteous, she encouraged me to give it a try, but wasn't promising anything. The editors of the other two villages would also have to approve anything I wrote.

That first piece generated enough positive response to generate a second and a third.

In the five years that followed, I had the unusual freedom of writing pretty much what I wanted and finding it in print word for word. My writing became very personal at times as I shared the pains of growing up (yes, even in middle age!). Only twice did Mags and the others think my subjects inappropriate. Whenever I thought readers might be tired of my observations and little philosophies, I would be admonished to continue. I learned that my column was being sent to friends and relatives. I heard more than once 'It's the first thing I turn to.'

When it came time to leave England, my grief threatened to swallow me whole. I wondered whether *A Yank* could engage a wider readership. So, I put the 60 odd columns into book form and sent 25 unsolicited manuscripts to as many publishers. Only one seemed to think my book had potential, one that also wanted some of my money. Was it worth the risk over the vain idea my words might matter to a paying public?

I hope my writings reflect the intensity of my love affair with Great Britain. It was that love that ultimately validated my decision to go ahead with the book; it was one way I could keep the threads of a relationship with England still woven in the present cloth of my life in California. I wish to thank Mags Fenn, Katherine Stonex, Gill Webb, Katie Thomas and John Giddings of *The Old Mail* staff for their permission to reprint my columns. Additional thanks go to The Book Guild staff, my copy editor, Debra Munn, and illustrator David Johnson.

My appreciation goes to the The University of Georgia Press, Athens, Georgia, for allowing me to adapt *The Untidy Girl*, a story told by Ruth Casey for the book *Storytellers – Folktales and Legends from the South*, edited by John A. Burrison.

Thanks to Lotty Spurrell, the talented teen who allowed me to include 'Ye Big Mac'.

I am also grateful to Earl Spencer, a man I met in passing, who not only took the time to read my manuscript, but gave me much more than the kind word I asked for. Thanks to Marianne Bicket for her intercession on my behalf.

And what would I have done without the support of my British cohorts Stephi Oates, Liz Robinson, Anne Watt of the Sheep, Phil Molloy, Phil Tipper, Niki Thomas and Shirley Whirley McClements, who always saw the good in me when I couldn't see it in myself?

To my parents, Marge and Dan Lewandowski, my husband, Jack Cosgrove, and my sons, Bill, Scott, Chris and Mark, thanks for allowing me to lovingly exploit you. Ditto to Mary Lavery and my friend Patricia Baron.

One last thank you. A short time before I left England, I was given a unique goodbye by the Friends of Paulerspury School, an organisation to which I had given some service while my son was a pupil there. I was given two identically-wrapped packages and asked to open just one. Inside was a wind chime that played *Chicago Blues*. But it was taken from me to be hung on the new school playground as a reminder of the special relationship we shared. The second package contained an identical chime. I was to take this one home with me and find a special place to hang it. The melody of the *Chicago Blues* drifts across my patio every day and eases the pain of separation from my second home. I swear that, if I listen closely, I can also hear the strains of *Rule Britannia*. And that's a fact!

Foreword

I first came across Linda Lewandowski on a miserable summer's evening in her adoptive English village, when the community was gathered to witness the completion of long-anticipated work on the school playground. After the more predictable parts of the proceedings, there was a surprise announcement that there was to be an honouring of someone who had been hugely important to everyone present, but who was sadly going home, to the States.

Linda came forward, deeply moved by the thoughtfulness of her neighbours, and overcome by the emotion of it all. I wondered then how somebody who had spent a transient period in a relative backwater in the English Midlands could have made such a deep impression on it. It doesn't happen very often: usually it takes at least a decade to forge such bonds in villages which, more and more, house commuters, pensioners and busy mothers; where, in short, a sense of community is often hard to forge.

Reading *A Yank in the Village*, it is easy to see why Linda settled in so well: keenly observant, yet never cruel or critical; intelligently perceptive, but not arrogant or condescending; richly humorous, while still self-effacing and accepting – these are glorious vignettes, weaving the familiar with the less obvious to make a deeply satisfying whole. Each chapter is a fascinating contribution from someone who is, by her very nature, a true contributor.

Earl Spencer

New Girl in Town

When, in early April, my family was given the chance to live in England for a few years, I fantasised about life in a small English village. Romantic notions planted in my youth by Jane Austen, the Brontë sisters and Thomas Hardy loomed large in my imagination. Lush countryside, rainy days and foggy nights with a 'cuppa' by the fire and a good book before retiring to a chilly bedroom under the covers with my love . . . Ah! Paradise!

Now it is August and, less than a week into my stay, I've encountered a dried-up countryside with relentless heat and sun. I have no time to read except for the owner's manuals for my 240-volt large and small appliances, and I retire to a bedroom covered with flies and hornets because I've left the unscreened windows open with the lights on. To top it off, my love (husband) and I are too tired from unpacking or too cross with each other from our different styles of unpacking to want to do much cuddling.

But it still feels like paradise to me in the form of a house called a 'Lawn', on a country estate outside a Northamptonshire village called Potterspury. I've never lived in a house without a number before. A product of American city and suburban cacophony, I pause often in my unpacking to marvel at the expansive farmland and flock of geese on the lake outside my window, and am tearfully grateful for new opportunities. A few days later, the continuous squawking of those geese on the lake reminds me of the never-ending screech of jet engines over my childhood home, nestled near the landing runway to John F. Kennedy airport.

Americans grow up with the peculiar notion, supported by media and government propaganda, that the USA is 'Number One' ... We're smarter, live better and build 'em bigger and better than any country in the world. I've always suspected that this was hogwash, but now I have a chance to evaluate this point of view from personal experience. Already I have so much I want to tell my friends back home about the aspects of British life I find innovative and efficient.

With typical Yankee assertiveness, I've convinced your editor to allow me to share the monthly musings of a 'registered alien' with you in your village newsletter. Having been placed in an area of England that is home to few Americans, I want to embrace the life here and make new friends who I hope will want to visit us in later years when we return to California.

So ... in future issues you may peruse such topics as 'Round-About in the Roundabout', 'The Tesco Trolley', 'BT and Me', 'My Friends at Currys' or 'Mommy, I Thought You Said They Spoke English Here' (from the mouth of my five-year-old son).

Many thanks to all who have extended the welcome mat to us and have challenged the stereotype of the reserved British citizen.

September '95

My Friends at Currys

'There is a principle which is a bar against all information, which is proof against all arguments and which cannot fail to keep a man in everlasting ignorance – that principle is contempt prior to investigation.'
Herbert Spencer

I have struggled with this in my first month in England as I make friends with the English toilet whose handle needs either a soft touch, a sharp push, several gentle jiggles or a combination of all three to function. And when I think I've finally got the hang of it, the handle that needed a sharp push suddenly wants several gentle jiggles. I'm also trying to find some merit in hard water as I notice little bits of debris floating in my coffee or vigorously rub out the spots on my drinking glasses.

Mostly I've been enamoured of my new discoveries – the ingenious 'airing cupboard', mail that arrives at 9.00 a.m., radio and TV not overrun with advertisements, lemon squash, the heated towel rack and, especially, the warmth and friendliness of the Britons I have met. From the London cabbie to the clerk in the petrol station, to the stranger I've asked for directions, to people in the villages, every one of them debunks the stereotype of cold, British reserve I've often heard about in the States. I want to focus on my friends at Currys, perhaps because acts of 'corporate' kindness seem so hard to find.

Making our house feel like home took on primary importance in my early days here. My husband often passed by

the Riverside shopping centre in Northampton on the way to work so we sought to buy what we needed from there. The transition from 110 to 240 volts necessitated the purchase of nearly all our electrical appliances and gadgets. Displays of items manufactured by companies I was unfamiliar with and sorting through their different aspects overwhelmed me (in my state of jet lag) all out of proportion. When a shining-faced boy, an obviously new sales clerk who couldn't have been more than 18 years old, tried to explain the merits of one washing machine over another, the manager at Currys wisely steered me to a woman of my own age who had obviously done a lot of laundry in her time. She counselled me according to my needs, helped me through the myriad of toasters, kettles and blenders and, later, when a glitch in communication botched up the washer delivery date, she straightened it out immediately.

In subsequent days, I also had need of the repair desk to sort out what I had done wrong in hooking up my US audio and TV equipment I had hoped to use here with the aid of transformers. The stock boys graciously hauled in everything I brought in, and the service people replaced fuses, gave instruction on how to properly change plugs where necessary and one even told me of a place to purchase an inexpensive tape deck to replace the one I totally messed up. That would never have happened in the States, folks. I would have had to fill out several forms, agree to pay a minimum inspection fee and not expect to see the items again for two weeks.

But the best part of all this is yet to come. My five-year-old son Mark, also in the throes of jet lag, usually accompanied me on these trips either half or totally asleep. When I mentioned I had to go to Harveys next door to shop for curtains, they suggested I let him sleep on the settee he had already found near the repair desk so I could shop in peace. I could have kissed them all. Concern for me was greater than their worry about possible litigation if Mark rolled onto the floor.

October '95

The Return of the Fly

I had intended to write about driving in the UK this time, but it occurred to me that my experiences have all been had before and described already by other people much funnier than I. What more could I say about a newcomer's reaction to the roundabouts, narrow lanes and the 'wrong' side of the road that hasn't been said already? Roundabouts are actually very efficient ways of moving traffic, roads would be narrow in a country old enough to have been graced by soldiers from the Roman Empire and 'wrong' could just as easily be called 'opposite'. And, after the initial shock of the higher speeds, I was surprised to find my own speedometer top 90 mph one day on the M1 and that I was loving every minute of it.

We're really not all that different. The Tory and 'New' Labour platforms sound remarkably similar to those of USA Republicans and Democrats and just as corruptible by human failing and greed. Tales of lottery fever, of murder and perversion, of the tarnished haloes of heroes and the newfound heroism of the commoner abound in the London *Times* just as in the *New York Times*. We love to laugh and enjoy the company of our friends. We rejoice at birth and grieve at death. We bemoan the spending power of the pound and the dollar. We struggle to find peace in a chaotic world. We fail to scoop up the dog poop.

I've moved around a lot in the States and learned from each move that, no matter how hard I've tried to dump them in the tip with the rest of the junk, those baffling bits of baggage I've termed my character flaws and moral dilem-

mas still find their way into the shoes and socks and pots and pans. Surely this time they wouldn't follow me across the Atlantic! What delusion! The following is a good illustration.

I have a basic belief that all life is sacred, and that my highly developed brain does not guarantee me any more of God's affection than, say, a fly. Yet, when I opened my son's bedroom door the other day and was greeted by hundreds of flies and that goddess of all bugs, the ladybird, and when opening the windows released hundreds more from the cracks, I had absolutely no hesitation in running to the village store for two cans of insecticide. I was relieved when the items were bagged, feeling as if I had purchased pornographic magazines. And when my son opened the windows of another room later that evening to get some air and was besieged by hundreds more bugs like in a grade 'C' horror film, and it turned out that nearly every window in the house harboured the same creatures, I dashed out for three more cans. Every bit of mist I inhaled I felt I deserved, for even the lowest human form would not kill a *ladybird*. Another case of expediency overcoming my principles. (Republican or Democrat?)

The next day I observed my two newly adopted dogs very happily chasing a distraught pheasant in my garden. Was their night a restless one, burdened by guilt for momentarily creating such havoc?

November '95

Bits and Pieces

The other day I received a notice from L. E. French at British Telecom that she had 'just received information from your local telephone exchange indicating that your next bill may be higher than your previous one and thought I should let you know right away'. Now I knew we were going to have a big bill due to all the calls to the states I had made, but never expected such a courteous warning from a utility. I'd like to think that out of her own innate goodness Mrs French was attempting to prevent a heart attack when I opened the imminent bill, but I suspect she realised heart failure would just delay payment.

Supermarkets here are much kinder to their checkout clerks than their counterparts in the States. They get to sit down while working, are not required to pack up your purchases or carry them out to your car for you. But those behind the meat counter are not so lucky. They have to wear those odd little hats!

Speaking of supermarkets, the first time I saw the locking trolley, I marvelled at British ingenuity. What a fabulous guarantee that the store would get their trolleys back in the racks instead of left all over the car park or sometimes even blocks away like you find them in the States. In fact, you will often find even the nicest American cars suffering from the 'shopping cart ding' syndrome caused by marauding trolleys rolling around unattended due to most Americans' aversion to walking. But nobody would let a dollar or a pound go to save a few steps. Except my husband! It took Jack two months to realise that you *do* get the money back

when you lock up the trolley again and his pound was not just given for the privilege of shopping at Tesco's. Oh! The lucky shoppers who happened upon those trolleys Jack had just surrendered! It must be a tribute to the British penchant for order that even in the markets where locking trolleys are no longer used, I still find trolleys neatly returned to the storage racks.

Did you know that it's a common American practice to add chlorine bleach to white laundry to get it clean enough? It's usually sold in 1 or 2 gallon bottles and is what you would call the 'thin' type. When I tried to find this in the stores I was asked 'why would you put *that* in your *wash*?' I was perplexed by this until I used my new washing machine for the first time and discovered that you get your wash clean by *boiling* your laundry. Whereas many washers here have a variety of choices of water temperatures controlled by the machine, American-made ones usually restrict you to 'hot', 'warm' or 'cold' solely controlled by the temperature of your tap water. *Nobody* in the States keeps their hot water at 90 degrees Celsius.

Cheers! is my favourite word in Britspeak. A magnificent upbeat all-purpose greeting surpassing *Hello! Good-bye! Thank you!* and *Good luck!* in its simplicity. I've only recently started to use it myself and after feeling a little silly saying it with the defined 'r' of my accent, it's beginning to bounce off the tongue and when I return to the States for the holidays I hope to brighten the surroundings with a little *Cheers!* instead of the now much-satirised and overused 'Have a nice day!'

Merry Christmas and a Happy New Year!

December '95

Behind the Wheel

I'm ready to write about driving now. I'm taking the exam for my British driving licence on February 15th.

As I look inward to find some explanation for why my resentment at having to do this knows no bounds, I reluctantly must admit that I hate being branded by the 'Scarlet Letter'! It's one thing to see a teenager behind the wheel plastered with letter 'L's and 'Remember, you were once a learner too' signs. But a 45-year-old woman with 27 years of driving experience and who has seen several cars safely into their sunset years? What a pain! A waste of time! A waste of money! A nuisance!

Now, rationally speaking, I know that I will become a better driver by learning roundabout etiquette and appreciating the differences between pelicans and zebras. Manoeuvreing a gearshift on the left side and grasping the ins and outs of a two-lane road with an 'imaginary' middle passing lane are helpful skills to master. But the frequent use of the handbrake at short stops and the practice of checking one's rearview mirror prior to making any stop both drive me crazy. As if a tailgater licking my rear would prevent me from stopping to avoid hitting the jaywalker in the pelican!

My teacher is very patient with my poor attitude. The first thing I said to him as I entered his car was 'I resent this whole thing. Please put up with me while I get used to this.' After four lessons, we're doing OK. Occasionally, there is a subtle tension when I say 'Well, in the States we do it this way . . .' as he retorts very calmly, 'Well, if you want to pass

your test, you must do it this way...'. That usually shuts me up.

There is one aspect of learning to drive British that is yet another example to me of how truth is often arbitrary in life – the art of turning. Allow me to take you back to the spring of 1968 in Ozone Park, New York City.

The following instructions were given to me by my driver's education teacher (DET) as the safest way to make a turn:

DET: Avoid the push-pull method of turning. Although under most circumstances, holding your hands at the 10.00 and 2.00–3.00 positions on the steering wheel is the safest, turning that way is clumsy, especially while coming out of your turn. The proper way to make a turn is to turn the wheel in the desired direction in a smooth motion, crossing hand over hand until the turn is completed and then allowing the wheel to slide gently back through your hands to its straight position as the car will tend to do automatically. We want to emphasise safety here. And you will be marked down on your test if you fail to execute a proper turn.

Contrast this with the instruction given to me by my British driving teacher (BDT):

BDT: The proper way to make a turn is to keep your hands in the 10.00 and 2.00–3.00 position. We want both hands on the wheel at all times. Never cross your hands or allow the wheel to slide through your hands as you are coming out of the turn. You are the one in control. We want to emphasise safety here. And you will be marked down on your test if you fail to execute a proper turn.

Pilate saith 'What is truth?' (St. John)

February '96

The Unlikely Ambassador

There's a popular phrase among social activists in the States – 'Think globally, act locally.' After years of trying to fit into organised movements designed to change bureaucracies and then only to feel overwhelmed and confused, I have come to see that the biggest part I can play in rectifying the injustices in the world is to be a fair, honest and just person myself with all the people I meet in my very ordinary daily life. So, it was with great trepidation and a strong sense of responsibility that I came to the United Kingdom as an unofficial United States ambassador. In an area of England that contains few Americans, I didn't want to be one of the stereotypical 'ugly' Americans who knows it all and has no patience with different ways of doing things.

I have been very conscious of alienating people by my ignorance of your customs or by making erroneous assumptions. It was an erroneous assumption that recently got me into trouble.

I have been enrolled in a class this winter on life in Roman Britain. Last week, several of us went up to the Cotswolds to visit the Chedworth Roman Villa and the Roman town of Cirencester. My first venture into what I had heard was a lovely area, I appreciated being able to ride with our tutor so I could enjoy the scenery. It was an extremely cold day and, as we viewed the remains of the Roman baths at Chedworth, we marvelled at the genius of Roman engineering and wished we could jump in a hot tub ourselves.

I neglected to bring a sack lunch as advised because I was running around like a chicken without a head that morning and *assumed* I could find something to buy. No such luck, but a kind classmate took care of me with an extra lunch she had.

After lunch we headed to Cirencester. After viewing the remains of the wall of the ancient city, we headed towards the centre of town and the museum there. We parked the cars on a busy street, where I decided to leave my handbag behind, which I *assumed* would be fine since my tutor had a car alarm and we were on such a busy street. Besides, this was an English town in the beautiful countryside, not New York City.

Ninety minutes later we came back to the car to find that the rear window had been smashed in and my handbag stolen. The thieves did not appear to be interested in the backpack or lunch bag also sitting on the rear seat. How could this have happened in broad daylight on a major thoroughfare with plenty of foot traffic? As I was lamenting my loss and the plight of my poor tutor who needed to leave quickly to teach an evening class, I suddenly realised with a sick feeling in my stomach that while I was not responsible for the evil that men do, I was at fault for putting out the 'Welcome' mat. If only I had carried the blasted thing with me! If only I had hidden it in the boot! Why was I stupid enough to leave it where it could easily be seen? Indeed, once my tutor knew why thieves were attracted to his particular vehicle in a long line of many left undisturbed, he turned to me with the restrained comment 'Silly girl!' He probably was really thinking 'XM@#*!^&*+~!!!!' When I offered to cover the excess on his motor insurance, there were no polite refusals, but one 'Thank you. That's very kind.'

By this time it was 4.30 p.m. and any hope of my tutor getting home in time to teach his class surely died when he found out that the auto glass company could not reach us until after 6.00 p.m. It was so cold that driving back with extra air-conditioning was not an option. After calls to the police and many more phone calls to cancel my switch card and credit cards, with borrowed money from my tutor and a classmate, we waited for the glass people. I offered to go for coffee or tea to warm us up (of course with my friends' money) in a vain attempt to ease the pain of frozen toes and noses, when the glass man arrived at 6.45 – with the wrong glass. It was after 8.00 p.m. when we finally began our journey home.

I had a further hour and a half to contemplate the damage I had done to Anglo-American relations as strains of a favourite Beethoven symphony from the car stereo failed to ease my embarrassment. People often relay misfortunes such as burglaries to friends and neighbours, and I envisioned my tutor's rendition of his fate as innocent victim of an horrendous afternoon either as 'This stupid *woman* left her handbag in plain sight as an invitation to violate my car' or 'This stupid *American* left her handbag in plain sight as an invitation to violate my car.' Neither alternative is easy to swallow but, in all fairness, honesty and justice, both are true.

On a positive note, I passed my British driving test. I just have to wait for the duplicate licence to arrive. The original was part of the stolen goods.

April '96

Ameri-Speak Quiz

Since summer is approaching, I offer those of you vacationing in the States some help with understanding Ameri-Speak. Match the 'British' words or phrases on the left with their corresponding 'American' translations on the right, and you'll have no trouble making yourself understood across the pond.

(answers provided below)

Ameri-Speak Quiz (travel version)

a.	bonnet	1.	chips
b.	Marmite	2.	teller
c.	WC	3.	highway or freeway
d.	boot	4.	911
e.	roundabout	5.	trunk
f.	zebra, pelican, puffin	6.	station wagon
g.	paracetamol	7.	elevator
h.	faggot	8.	Mickey D's
I.	plaster	9.	subdivision
j.	bank clerk	10.	clinic, doctor's office
k.	999	11.	hood
l.	serviettes	12.	bus
m.	spanner	13.	Republican
n.	lift	14.	no such recognisable substance
o.	tube	15.	Band-Aid
p.	estate	16.	exit or intersection
q.	McDonald's	17.	meatball
r.	postcode	18.	traffic circle (few and far between)

s. Tory
t. crisps
u. flat
v. junction
w. coach
x. housing estate
y. motorway
z. surgery

19. ped Xings
20. apartment
21. zip code
22. wrench
23. acetaminophen
24. restroom
25. napkins
26. subway

A Word of Warning: If you don't get 'z' right you're apt to be wheeled into an operating theatre for removal of a body part you don't really want to lose.

ANSWERS:

a) 11, b) 14, c) 24, d) 5, e) 18, f) 19, g) 23, h) 17, i) 15, j) 2, k) 4, l) 25, m) 22, n) 7, o) 26, p) 6, q) 8, r) 21, s) 13, t) 1, u) 20, v) 16, w) 12, x) 9, y) 3, z) 10

May '96

Down on the Farm

The closest I ever got to living in a rural setting prior to my move to England was a magical month spent in the cornfields surrounding a small town in the US midwest in the summer of 1971. Imlay City, Michigan, was known as 'The Gateway to the Thumb', a rather bewildering distinction until you look at the shape of the state that for so many years has been the hub of the American auto industry. If you look at your right hand palm side up, you are roughly looking at the state of Michigan. Imlay City is right there in your hand as you head out towards the thumb.

 As lively a hippie as there ever was, I was excited to be down on the farm and back to nature, though the time spent in my friend's well-worn farm house mostly consisted of marathon card-playing sessions while consuming gallons of soft drinks, eating impressive quantities of junk food and watching soap operas on TV while we were supposed to be fixing up the house. We did our share of skinny-dipping in the mushy-bottomed pond out back to the strains of the Rolling Stones and Bob Dylan and ushered in the wee hours of the mornings with self-righteous discussions on the state of the world.

 The town itself was not much more than a block long and consisted of the small 'Mom and Pop' stores that could service your basic needs quite well until you needed that special dress or service only an urban area could supply. It was with great wonder that this 'little goil from Brooklyn' began to see that there was another world out there away from the big city.

My husband and I were married in Imlay City (pronounced *Emily*), as his folks from the west coast and mine from the east coast met for the first time to celebrate their offsprings' decision to quit living in sin. We had the best little wedding in the local church amid speculation that the ceremony might have been encouraged by a soon to emerge bundle of joy which would inevitably cause our divorce. In actuality, our little bundle did not appear until five years later and what the folks really observed was the beginnings of my own chronic battle of the bulge. No, our wedding was mostly the practical result of realising that Jack's mom and dad would not tolerate our sharing a room together on our impending visit if we had not officially tied the knot. Over time, my father has spent many an evening telling friends the story of our wedding and how he 'got away cheap'.

Twenty-five years and four sons later, after living all over the USA from Boston to Dallas to Atlanta to San Francisco, we find ourselves celebrating our silver wedding anniversary year in small-town England, the land of the country village with a lively pulse of activity all its own. My first reaction is 'How have I gotten to be so old so fast? I don't even *have* any silver.' All of those old clichés that I resented as a youth, about youth being wasted on the young and if-I-only-knew-then-what-I-know-now, now have a familiar resonance. The older I get, the stupider I feel and my parents, who certainly didn't know much about anything when I was 18, now seem endowed with extraordinary wisdom.

By the way, my folks are soon to arrive for a six-week visit. So if you see a distinguished older man with white hair and a Florida-tanned face driving a grey Volvo Estate on the wrong side of the road on his way to the village shop to get a newspaper, please be kind.

June '96

A Postscript: When my parents arrived, I enthusiastically gathered all my Old Mail *articles together to proudly show off my 'published' work. I waited in excited anticipation as* would a reception class pupil upon presentation of her first sentence. Oh! The praise I would receive!

The first comment came from Mother:
'Don't you think you're getting a little too personal here? I mean, some of this is really private.'

From my Dad:
'Whaddya mean "I got off cheap?" I never said that.'

As my shoulders slumped and I looked dejectedly down at the floor, lower lip protruding, I suddenly remembered why I never showed them my writing when I was young. I guess a kid never stops trying to please her parents, even when she's nearly 46 years old.

Bumper Stickers

For as long as my husband remains assigned to his job in England, his company provides us with annual transportation back to the States to renew family ties and friendships, take care of personal business and, in general, avoid the homesickness that can sabotage an overseas commitment.

As we left the San Francisco airport in our rental car for our home visit, and eased into the heavy freeway traffic, I noticed a bumper sticker on the car ahead which read 'The next time you think you're perfect, try walking on water.' As I glanced about me in the California sunshine and saw a variety of the 4″ by 12″ stickers which frequently adorn cars in the States, I thought 'Wow! I'm really home!' Where else but in America would people turn their love affair with the automobile into a forum for political, social and spiritual commentary?

Now, I've done a fair amount of driving in the UK and have noticed an occasional 'A puppy is not just for Christmas' or an allegiance to a favourite radio station or sports team, but never have I seen anything like 'Roses are red, violets are blue, I'm schizophrenic and so am I.' (I kid you not.)

Throughout my five-week stay, I researched this bit of Americana and present the following selection of Bumper Sticker Wisdom to you without opinion as to content or political correctness:

If you can read this,
You're driving too close.

God said it.
I believe it.
That settles it.

*You toucha my car,
I breaka you face*

Higher-Powered

Minds are like parachutes.
They only function when open.

I owe, I owe.
It's off to work I go.

Proud Parent of a
(any name) School
Honor Student

My kid beat up your
Honor Student.

My Other Car is a Horse

*It will be a great day when our
schools get all the money they
need, and the Air Force has to hold
a bake sale to buy a bomber.*

*You cannot simultaneously plan
for and prevent war.
Albert Einstein*

If you think education is expensive,
TRY IGNORANCE!

SMART BOMBS or
SMART KIDS?
Put your money where
our future is!

HONK!
If You Love America!

September '96

Do I Miss the USA?

When I am introduced to new people here, they often ask me what I miss most about home. Of course I miss the intimacy of having close friends about. You all know the kind of friends I'm talking about. Those one or two blessed souls who still love you even when they find out you secretly pick your nose or might not wash your hands after every trip to the toilet. The kind you can barge in on with your crying kids in tow, whose settee you collapse on tearfully and to whom you scream 'Put the kettle on. I'm having a nervous breakdown!!!' and they'll drop everything to do just that. Fortunately, some of my new British friends are becoming just like them.

Other things I miss are not as important, but are more related to convenience. Such as day and night telephone banking. While I have this service here now, it initially took a bit of doing to obtain.

24-Hour Banking by Touchtone Telephone is an automatic service which is provided to everyone in the USA with an account, no matter how large or small. It is not a 'special' service like I discovered here, requiring a separate application or bank management approval. If you question the need for such a service, read on.

Situation #1
You are at your desk or kitchen table one evening, paying your bills by cheque after the children are in bed, and you notice that you have made a record-keeping error. Your current account is overdrawn by the cheque you wrote to

the dry cleaners today unless you transfer funds from your savings account. Since your bank has 24-hour phone banking service, you dial the number (usually a freephone), follow the recorded security instructions to weed out impostors who might be impersonating you, then do the transaction with your touchtone phone. Voilà! You've avoided a trip to your branch office the next day.

Situation #2
You are reviewing your 15th of September statement posted to you by your bank on the following Sunday afternoon, and are verifying that your cheque stub notations match the bank's accounting. You have been sloppy in your record-keeping and notice that you forgot to note the last two cheques you wrote. Now, who did you write them to, what were those dates, how much were they for? You get on the 24-hour phone line, punch in those pesky cheque numbers to see if they have cleared, and find that the first was written in the amount of £1.99 and cleared on the 18th, jarring your memory of your child's school book order form that you turned in at the last minute. Though the automated bank clerk tells you that the other cheque still hasn't cleared, you remember writing it to the milkman the same day as the book order day as you were hurrying out the door to walk your child to school.

Situation #3
Your daughter at university has a student account which she keeps funded partially by her part-time job, and partially by you. You have access for paying-in only. Rather than writing and posting her monthly allowance cheques to her, you transfer funds from your account to hers by phone. She phones you late one evening saying that her maths professor wants her to purchase a special calculator. The university shop has one left, but it is expensive and will deplete her account for that month. Since her request for additional money sounds reasonable and you have some extra money this month, you tell her you will arrange for

the transfer of funds by phone and that she'll have the money the next day.

It might seem like I'm doing a 24-hour banking advert. But this is merely an illustration of Americans' love of creature comforts and why we are often rightly perceived as impatient when we travel abroad. Next month I'll take you to Kinko's 24-hour printing shop, Caffino's drive-thru gourmet coffee kiosk and Costco shopping warehouse.

October '96

The REAL Superstore

As the largest consumer population in the world, Americans demand value, convenience and service. Shopping warehouses, originally developed for the merchant, restaurant owner or business person to purchase large quantities of their supplies at a discount, have been opened to the general public and, in the past ten years, have grown in popularity. The closest thing you have here is Bookers Cash and Carry, but you must still be a retailer or charity to use it, and you must set a limit on how much you will spend per week there if you pay by cheque.

The actual physical size of these places is formidable. If you took the Homebase store in Milton Keynes and raised the roof, you might have the space of a Costco. Jam-packed with shelves from floor to ceiling, the store organises the lower shelves to carry the items for immediate sale, with the higher shelves reserved for storage. The range of items is equally intimidating. Large and small appliances, housewares, furniture, TVs, VCRs, stereo equipment, cameras and computers, including software, dominate one section. Not all brands are represented, just the ones the store can get the best deals on. But there are usually good name-brands. Clothing, shoes, office supplies, garden equipment, toys, sporting goods, books, CDs, videos and auto supplies, including tyres, are available. Cosmetics, pet supplies, sodas, the usual range of goods you find in the supermarket, paper goods, fresh and frozen meats and fish, produce, spirits and cigarettes abound. There is often a bakery, and sometimes even a fine jewellery counter. And, if you get hungry from

all this shopping, there are workers nestled in the food aisles giving you free samples of the newest lines of food and drink the store may offer.

In order to shop here, you must be a member. An annual fee of about $35 (£22) per family or business is common. The amount you save over regular store prices in just one shopping trip can offset that fee. The other catch is that you must buy small items in quantity. If you need ketchup, you might have to buy three bottles. If you need butter, you might have to buy four pounds of it. Ten pounds of mince, 50 pounds of dog food, six rolls of film, a gallon of mayonnaise, a dozen pairs of socks, a case of soda, a 12-ounce jar of powdered garlic. Most people who shop at the Costco have a large refrigerator with a separate freezer, and often store extra items in their garages.

The seductive character of these stores is powerful. Even the shopping trolleys are huge and, with the merchandise practically screaming at you 'Buy! Buy! Buy!' it is easy to spend a paycheque in 30 minutes. If you are a prudent shopper, one who always uses lists, budgets carefully each month and is not prone to impulse buying, a monthly or biweekly stop at the Costco will result in substantial savings for you. I know a family with seven children who would be hard-pressed to feed themselves at regular store prices. However, if you have trouble managing money, the Costco can be a dangerous place for overspending on things you could better do without.

To be continued...

November '96

Since this writing I have discovered that there are seven Costco stores in England, with membership restricted to retailers and certain professionals. The Watford store has many US expat members from the large American community in Surrey.

LL, November '98

The 24-Hour Office

It's midnight and I'm at the computer designing *Old Mail* adverts to be given to John Giddings the next day. Suddenly my printer refuses to process the advert I've just completed. When all my tricks fail to solve the problem, I wistfully think about Kinko's back home.

Kinko's is a nationwide chain of shops advertised as 'Your Office Away from the Office'. Open 24 hours a day, 365 days a year, it offers professional printing services to meet any need.

If Kinko's was down the road, I could transfer my adverts on to a computer disk, jump in the car and, for a small fee, use a compatible self-service computer there to print my ads. And should I need to do any additional cut and paste work to add any graphics wanted by the *Old Mail* advertiser, I could spread out my work on a large Kinko's work station complete with glue, scissors, correction tape and fluid, staplers, paper clips and guillotine to get it copy-ready.

With that done, I'd obtain a special copier 'key' to activate one of the dozen or so self-service photocopiers. With the key accounting for the number of copies I made, I'd go about my business, return the key to a young and cheerful clerk certainly trained by flight attendants, and pay up. I don't pay for errors and prices begin at 4 cents (2.75p) for a single A4-sized copy and decrease with volume copying.

Say I wanted to turn an ad publicising a Christmas Fayre into a giant poster. A Kinko's clerk would enlarge it in any

colour up to 30"×36", then laminate it for under $5.00 (£3.25).

Passport photos, business cards, wedding invitations, customised stationery, use of typewriters and a small selection of office supplies are all available at Kinko's. During daytime hours, the shop is apt to be jammed with customers.

Now should I leave the shop between the hours of 7 a.m. and 9 p.m. and desire a cup of coffee, I might stop at Caffino's or the Java Express, drive-thru kiosks offering premium coffees in a travel cup with a leak-proof lid and straw to boot. A double-decaf (16 oz.) cinnamon cappucino or a double cafe mocha with whipped cream and chocolate sprinkles would cost me $3.00 (£1.75). A single raspberry-flavoured cafe latte would cost me $2.00 (£1.25). I can also buy a plain old French Roast or Amaretto-flavoured coffee for a buck. While I think that it would be a great idea to open a Caffino's on the A5, I wonder whether my British friends in the country would be willing to pay those prices for a cup of coffee.

This is the last of the three-part series about things I sometimes miss away from home. I certainly don't long for them enough to want to return to life in the States. And, after fifteen months in Potterspury, I've come to love the unique quality of village life that nurtures the soul of this Yank.

December '96

Yuletide Bits and Pieces

Christmas Crackers ... Last year I thought these were biscuits shaped like Christmas trees and angels that you ate with the Stilton and Port. When I was set straight I still didn't buy any, because I was lugging enough pressies back to the States as it was. Since we were spending this Christmas in England, I knew I had to have some this year, but when I went to the shops I was overwhelmed by the cracker displays: Christmas Crackers, Classic Christmas Crackers, Family Christmas Crackers, Deluxe Christmas Crackers, Luxury Christmas Crackers, Super Luxury Christmas Crackers, down to Mini Christmas Crackers. Where should I buy them, I asked? Are Toys 'R Us, Woolies or Tesco brands tacky crackers? Are Marks & Spencer's luxury any better than Clifford's? Should I do the make-your-own variety? In the end, I decided to splurge since this was my first Christmas here and bought two boxes of beautifully appointed W. H. Smith's Super Luxury at 20 quid a box, as well as some DIYs. The DIYs I never did get around to filling, and I forgot to put the others on the Christmas dinner table. When, a few days later, some friends came over for an impromptu dinner, I excitedly put them out. One little girl waxed ecstatic at the four brocaded lipstick holders with mini mirrors given to her by the boys who found them in their crackers. My ceramic salt & pepper shakers were cool and someone else got a great pen. But we didn't play the charade game and several hats remained unfolded. Next year, I'll make time for the DIYs! ... Back home, *Mince Pies* are usually below the pumpkin pies,

pecan pies and cheesecakes and just above the fruit cake in popularity as holiday sweets. After being saturated with them here, I realise that the secret of a good mince pie is a *mini* mince pie ... I was glad to hear that *Boxing Day* was not the day you put the kids in opposite corners of the room, admonish them to fight clean and, then, at the sound of the gong, watch them duke it out for three rounds over the best Christmas presents! ... I had the best *New Year's Eve* with the Paulerspury Players who booked their village hall for their annual do. Adults and children shared a great communal supper, then were entertained by various Players until the anticipated midnight hour. The highlight for me was a gent on a keyboard who led a group sing which included 'Waltzing Matilda', 'Pack Up Your Troubles in Your Old Kit Bag' and 'It's a Long Way to Tipperary'. As I happily joined in, though I had to ask what a 'billabong' was, I remembered being entranced by all the old romantic films I had seen on TV in the 50s where the weary soldiers from the World Wars would trudge along bravely in the mud singing these songs. And here I was, a woman who had never known the sound of approaching warplanes as sirens wailed, who never had to be separated from Mom and Dad to be safe from the deadly cargo carried by those planes, and who never has seen her cities destroyed, singing along like a mate with new friends whose not so distant past included those very things. Though light-headed from libation, I was sobered by these thoughts as the clock struck 12, the balloons were released and we swayed to the sounds of 'Auld Lang Syne'.

February '97

School

As PTA chairman at the Paulerspury School, as a classroom volunteer there, and in plying my storytelling trade throughout the schools in the surrounding villages, I have spent a lot of time within these schools during the school day. Since I have always been an active volunteer at my children's schools, it has been interesting to note the differences I see in both educational philosophy and social atmosphere between these small village schools and the ones I've known back home.

My initial reaction was one of dismay at the tiny classrooms and bare playgrounds. My impression that the teachers seemed more severe here also spawned an anxiety that my five-year-old's creativity might be stifled. But the more time I spent at school, the more I saw that the children as a whole seemed pretty happy. Yes, there are times when pupils are expected to be completely quiet, but there is a greater tolerance of noise during those times when they work together. The kids don't seem to notice the lack of elaborate playground equipment. They seem to delight in playing tag, jumping rope, kicking around the football and just hanging out. My son, Mark, came home one day, exasperated by the game of 'kissy-chase', where squealing little girls tag you with a kiss. I'm not sure kissy-chase would be tolerated in politically correct America, where fears of sexual harassment lawsuits might prevail. And the children are given much more time to play here. Besides the 15 minutes of morning and afternoon playtime ('recess' as we call it back home), the children have a 1 hour and 15 minute

lunch break. The US schools my older sons, now 21, 18 and 16, attended allowed only 45 minutes, never enough time, to my mind, for the children to blow off steam.

The phonetic approach to reading here and the immediate immersion into seeing the alphabet in context of words and sentences has impressed me. When my older children began kindergarten in the States at age five, they learnt to pronounce their letters as 'Ay', 'Bee', 'Cee', 'Dee', 'Eee', 'Eff', etc. They might spend a whole week on one letter, writing that letter, seeing words that begin with that letter, but not seeing the relationship of words in sentences until much later in the year. Their daily homework might be to bring home a book for Mum or Dad to read to them, but they really are not encouraged to do their own reading until the first grade.

So I was amazed when, right from the beginning, Mark brought home a book to read, accompanied by a little tin of words. It took me awhile to get the hang of saying the letters more as they sound: 'Ah', 'Buh', 'Cuh', 'Duh', 'Ehh' 'Fuh', etc., and it seemed that the teacher was asking an awful lot from a little guy. Once I realised that the teacher was not expecting immediate mastery, I relaxed and began to see how quickly Mark progressed, and how good he felt at being able to read.

Soon I saw that each child was being treated as an individual, each being given the level of book and words he or she needed. I especially appreciated the sensitivity with which Mark was approached as a foreign pupil, as well as a first-time pupil. He wasn't pressured to do more than he felt comfortable with. As a five-and-a-half-year-old, he really should have been a year 1 instead of a reception class child like he was. This year he has moved on to the next class as a year 2, once the teachers assessed he could handle the extra work he would need to do to catch up. Since the class consists of a mixture of year 1 and 2 students, that kind of flexibility is easier to achieve. For some reason, American parents dislike mixed classes because they fear that the older children will be held back by too much focus on the younger ones, an attitude I never shared because I always thought it was good for the ages to mix.

When I began telling stories in the classrooms here, I noticed several children in each class getting comfy with their thumbs in their mouths, even a few nine or ten-year-olds. I kept waiting for a teacher to reprimand them for being babies, but none did. And then it struck me that right there was the main difference between your schools and the ones back home. You let your kids be kids longer. They seem to trust their adults more, are more innocent, feel safer and protected by their adults, are not pushed into academic or sporting competition too soon, are allowed to play more. And wearing uniforms to school keeps everyone on an even playing field. You wouldn't believe the mayhem that occurs in the States in getting the kids ready for 'Back to School'.

I suspect I might feel differently if I lived in the city. Because village schools are so small, they are more manageable both for the pupil and the teacher. It's so much easier to relate to 100 rather than 300 or 400 other people. My older sons went to primary schools in the States with up to 800 children, just too many bodies.

While I am most happy with Mark's little school, I can see that something gets lost here as children go through secondary school. You seem to have no shortage of disillusioned teenagers who feel drawn to alcohol and drug abuse, just like back in the States. Perhaps the information superhighway has made it more difficult for adults to pretend that age and experience automatically deserve respect, reducing the old 'Do as I say, even though I may do the opposite because I'm an adult' to even less credible proportions. Why, all kids have to do is press a button on the remote to find the Members of Parliament in behaviour which most primary school teachers would reward with a visit to the Head Teacher's office!

March '97

Time for a Whinge

In the American Declaration of Independence, we are told that all men are created equal, and that we are endowed by our Creator with the rights to life, liberty and the pursuit of happiness. Each morning, as I drive my son Mark to school in Paulerspury, I know I'm not in Kansas anymore and that I must be living somewhere over the rainbow, because no sane American driver would also endow himself with the right to pursue driving three abreast on the A5 at 60–70 miles per hour. Do you guys pay protection money to your guardian angels?

In my early days of UK driving, my husband warned me about A5 driving etiquette:

> 'Lin, you've got to watch out for the drivers coming up the middle lane to pass.'
> 'What middle lane?' I scoffed.
> 'You see those faded white broken lines? That's the middle lane.'
> 'You mean they don't wait for a clear stretch of road in my lane?'
> 'Many do, but some don't.'
> 'You're kidding, right? And surely no car would try to squeeze between two trucks?'
> 'Ha! You watch 'em,' he guffawed smugly.
> 'Well, where am I supposed to go, on the field with the sheep? I don't drive a 4×4, you know!'
> 'Baaa! Baaa!'

When I was working with my British driving teacher, I asked him about the 'third lane' and why it was marked so poorly. He explained that the road used to be marked as a three-lane road in parts for passing, but that the county relined it because it was deemed unsafe. The faded lines were remnants of the past. I also asked him why so many drivers passed across the solid lines and at junctions, if that was indeed illegal as he had previously warned. He gave me one of those looks my Dad used to give me when he would say: 'I don't *care* what Joe Blo does. You're *my* daughter and so you do the right thing.'

My favourite expletives are reserved for the driver who weaves his path like he's test-driving a Ferrari through an obstacle course. He's heading toward Milton Keynes at 8.30 a.m. in a slow-moving queue behind four cars which, in turn, are crawling behind a humongous Eddie Stobart. Those of us travelling in the opposite direction are doing 60 mph to his 35 mph. He's just got to pass that Stobart, totally disregarding the laws of motion and the capacity of his Escort to acclerate to 70 to make it past that truck before he becomes sandwiched between it and the P & O lorry in front of me. (And it is usually a *he* and not a *she*.)

Yes, he thinks. I think I can, I think I can, I think I can! But, what's this? My little engine that could, can't? I'll just cut back in front of that little Peugeot 106 behind the truck and try again near that straightaway by the Super Sausage Cafeteria. It won't matter at all that some mum with her two little toddlers might be waiting to turn right for the Wakefield Farm Shop to get some eggs. I am invincible! I am in control! I must save two seconds to get to work! Yes! Yes! I've done it.

No sooner does he pass the antique shop further up the road when he finds himself in another queue behind a Dixon's fuel tanker. His mantra fills his spirit once more. I think I can, I think I can, I think I can!

April '97

Reflections on Expatriation

I sit here recuperating from foot surgery with doctor's orders being no weight bearing activity for two weeks – no walking, no driving, just a teetering hobble on crutches for the basic shower and toilet runs while those near and dear cater to my every whim. What an opportunity for tax preparation, catching up on overdue correspondence, PTA organisation, goal planning! If only I could tear myself away from the mini electronic Yahtzee game in search of the always greater score.

Actually, what I need to focus on is my upcoming talk, 'An American Perspective of Britain', for a nearby Women's Institute meeting later this month. Perhaps a few members have gotten wind of these monthly *Old Mail* essays and have made the assumption I might have something profound to say – for *only* 45 minutes to an hour, the secretary informed me. It usually takes me about two hours to write an *Old Mail* column that probably takes you three minutes to read. Let's see! Sixteen columns so far. That's 48 minutes. Voilà!

The reality is that I don't think people should perceive me or my comments as coming from a typical American woman. Most Americans don't get or wouldn't want an opportunity for expatriate living. Those who do are usually given very nice moving packages to make it enticing enough to uproot the family and kids to a foreign country when they probably have been moved Stateside several times already due to Dad's or Mom's career. My older teenage boys only willingly came along to England when they knew

that Dad's company would fund the tuition for an American high school, which would prepare them for the university system back home and where they could continue to play basketball at the competitive level they were used to. They were willing to board five days a week in order to do so, since the school was south of London and Dad's job was in Northampton. (Boarding school is almost unheard of for secondary schoolers in the States. It's commonly thought of only as the option of the super rich who get rid of their kids so they can spend more time on their yachts!) It's taken Scott and Chris nearly two years to appreciate the doors that have been opened to them in their view of the world and in their own maturing process as a result of their move to England. And the experience has actually been very good for us as a family, because when we see each other on weekends we appreciate each other more and don't tend to bicker about the little things.

Most American expats employed by large corporations get financial help when they have to sell their cars and houses back home, have moving expenses paid and are given tax relief so they are not double-taxed. And most of them live in London or south of London with their children going to the American schools in the area. They hang out together, work on the PTA together, play together and sometimes work together to get the superstores to stock more American products. When I mentioned to a woman I met at a basketball game that after seven years in London she must feel like a real Briton, she said that most of her friends were other American expats.

I didn't want to move to England to hang around with other Americans most of the time. I had great fantasies of forming lasting friendships with some wonderful British families who would always feel welcome in my American home when the time came for me to return. Once I got over my reluctance to move *again*, I felt like a child entering the biggest and best toy store I could imagine. On every shelf there would be more to learn about. Would people really be that different? Would I be able to see more realistically the benefits of having grown up American as well as its liabilities? From the threshold of England would we be able to explore some of the rest of Europe if we were lucky? How could so many peoples with so many languages live so close together and try to get along? Will anybody like me? Will I have any friends?

I hope to tell the members of the Women's Institute that I have been humbled many times in the short time I have been here. That my impressions are mine alone and are not representative of all Americans. That my observations are shared with good humour and affection and with the notion that when we all stared with wonder at the Hale-Bopp Comet, we were all standing on the same planet.

May '97

Parenthood

When I was a child, I felt a kinship with my father, but at odds with my mother. She insisted on making me look like a dork while the other girls were hiking their skirts, teasing their hair, wearing nylons, plucking their eyebrows and wearing make-up. I had to wear Mary Janes when everyone else wore penny loafers. Mom worked hard to sew me clothes I was sure she would have worn during the world war. And at the slightest hint of rain, she made me wear a raincoat and boots which I stuffed into my book bag as soon as I rounded the corner to the bus.

I never had the kind of relationship with my mom that those TV sitcom teenagers had. *Late night talks after dates.* (I never had any dates even though I was thin in those days and considered reasonably attractive.) *Flinging myself into my mother's arms after a trying day at school for support.* (I usually retreated to my room with silent tears in my pillow.) *Intimate talks about sex, boys and womanly bodily functions.* (She did give me a book written by a nun called *20th Century Teenagers*, an anthology of horror stories. Like the one about the young couple entwined in death's embrace on a cold winter's night on Lovers' Lane as carbon monoxide's toxic vapours seeped in through the car's heater. The nun also knew for a fact that the mortal sin of 'self-abuse', while regrettably common in teenaged boys, was extremely rare in girls. I hated that book.)

I swore I would have a different relationship with my own daughter. That's probably why God gave me four sons. Admittedly, I aspired to a different style of parenting, more democratic, sensitive, open, avoiding the 'Because I'm your mother, that's why you do what I say!' explanation of my decisions. Flower power philosophy, linked to a strong foundation of honesty, integrity and responsibility, would be my path as a mother. Drug-free childbirth, long-term breast-feeding, open duvet policy for a frightened child needing comfort in Mom and Dad's bed; my role as defender and promoter of my children's well-being was so clear. I would look at those newspaper photos of devastated parents of convicted serial killers and be sure that their parenting was the real guilty party. Such is the self-righteousness of the inexperienced.

The older I get the more I sound like my mother.

'I don't have kids, I have pigs!'

'I'm not sure I want you to go to that concert. You'll get trampled by the weirdos.'

'How can you sleep with those headphones blasting that noise in your ears?'

'How many times do I have to tell you? Shut the freezer door.'

'Call me when you get there.'

'Your brother's five. You're 16. You should know better.'

'How long has it been since you've changed your underwear?'

'Are you listening to me? What am I doing? Talking to the wall? Hello, wall!'

'You call this kitchen clean???'

Sometimes I sound like my father.

'Hit the brake! Hit the brake! You trying to kill me?'

'Are you on drugs?'

In that last vein I have to share with you my most embarrassing moment as a parent, that one moment you wish you could take back but know you'll be tortured with at every subsequent family gathering for the rest of your life.

As a former experimental drug user in my hippie days, and eternally grateful for having survived while others didn't, I've been overly conscious of watching out for dilated

pupils, slurred speech and red, runny noses in my teenagers. When my 22-year-old was about 18 he had some friends over while I was out and, as I later sat on the patio, I noticed these little plastic tubes littering the pavement. I immediately thought of amyl nitrate containers, poppers we used to call them, the same stuff sometimes used to revive someone who has fainted. They came in little tubes, you 'popped' them in half and inhaled deeply for a big rush. Provided you didn't have heart problems, it was a kick that lasted a couple of minutes. I understand they are still part of today's drug culture.

When I confronted my son, he looked at me quizzically, told me I was crazy and that he didn't know what those tubes were. I mentioned that denial was a big symptom of drug abuse, and he angrily stormed off. I brooded and searched the patio to see how many tubes there were. As I did so, I found a bunch of papers in an adjacent room thick with white glue and the same amount of slightly larger tubes emblazoned with the bold letters *'Glue Stic'*. They looked remarkably similar to the ones I had recently purchased in bulk at the discount store. I had just accused my son of inhaling white, non-toxic, little-kids-could-safely-eat-without-fatality glue-paste! Of course it was my four-year-old and his friends who produced my incriminating evidence. Engulfed in *Glue Stic* mania, they dissected the cylinders when they were done.

When I realised my mistake, I immediately approached my 18-year-old in an effort to apologise for being an idiot. As he gazed in disbelief at my eyes welling with tears, he wasn't going to let me off that easy. He was angry that I had misjudged him and I can't really remember when he forgave me in the course of subsequent days. But when he stalked off, I called after him in a pleading voice very similar to a chastened child's:

'Are you going to tell Dad about this?'

I still wince when I think of this incident, which is often mentioned by my sons with humour and affection when I'm feeling absolutely sure of some opinion. There have been many other, less glaring perhaps, incidents in my 22 years of parenting imperfections that have rightly shrunk my ego. But it is this one in particular that grants me lifetime membership in that universal sisterhood of mothers who err in wanting to protect (or control) their children.

Despite what I would wish otherwise, my mistakes have turned me into a much better mother than my triumphs. They have brought me to love my own mother dearly and to recognise the magnitude with which she loved me as I was growing up. They have shown me the part my own personality played in keeping distant from her in my formative years. I'm grateful that her good health has given her a life long enough for me to make amends for my insensitivities as a daughter and to pamper her when I get the chance.

My 16-year-old son Chris broke both of his wrists last year in an absurd move to slam-dunk a basketball while leaping from a desk chair. Out of Chris's earshot, the school nurse whispered to me over the phone, 'He's said he wants his mum.' I guess I can't be all bad.

June–July '97

Hanging Up the Laundry

As I basked in the California sunshine last summer, and while viewing the suburban landscape, I reflected on the incongruity of being in a region where the sun shines continuously for five months out of the year and for much of the time the rest of the year and where one would be hard-pressed to find a clothesline. This in contrast to England, where Mrs Murphy's bloomers can always be seen flapping in the breeze, despite the fact that, in all likelihood, they will be rained on at the exact moment when they are completely dry. Now I've always loved the fresh smell and crisp countenance my cotton clothes and towels and sheets possess when dried by the sun and wind, and I often hang them up, but I have a strong aversion to the steam iron, and can't imagine what life would have been like raising four sons with voluminous amounts of cloth diapers without the tumble dryer. Actually, I do know what life would be like, since I've seen the piles and piles of ironing my women friends do here. I couldn't believe it when my friend told me she ironed her children's uniforms, T-shirts and boxer shorts. Her children must be much tidier than mine, who often take the clean laundry I've piled on their beds for them to put away and crumple it up as they shove it into their bureaus. And I have a hard time seeing the wisdom of spending so much time pressing a sleeve which will probably be covered with snot when my son uses it for a handkerchief or to wipe ketchup from his face when he needs a serviette.

There are some folks in America who are *not allowed* to hang up their laundry because it is against the CC & Rs

(Clauses, Covenants & Restrictions.). These are people who live in condominiums or planned housing developments which are notable for their homogeneous homes and gardens. These communities often have sparkling, supervised swimming pools and common park land which appeal to families and for which each homeowner must pay a monthly fee to maintain. Homeowners are members of a 'Home Owners Association' (HOA) whose elected representatives handle the management of the common ground and set guidelines for the overall atmosphere of the community.

That's where the CC & Rs come in. Some HOAs prohibit certain colours of house paint, some prevent you from attaching a basketball hoop to your house, others ban trash bins on the street for more than one night after the rubbish is picked up, some frown upon unsightly lawns, some will not allow an old jalopy your son might be refurbishing to be parked on the street and some prohibit the use of clotheslines. The idea of all of this is to keep the neighbourhood looking as upscale as possible so the property values stay high. Nice neighbours don't clutter the landscape with their britches or allow weeds to grow in their gardens.

In reality, it's not so bad because, even though there is usually a committee who does a drive-thru of the development once a month looking for violations, you really have to be an horrendous offender – paint your house black or have a skip in the driveway for a month – to get fined. And when you get down to the nitty-gritty, the six or so elected HOA representatives end up doing a lot of work while the five hundred other homeowners sit and gripe but never show up at the monthly meetings to help out or change things. Does that sound familiar, council members?

October '97

About Cake and Coffee

Whenever my British guests sample one of my white cakes (white because they are made with egg whites only) they invariably use the word 'gorgeous' to describe it. Coated with creamy vanilla icing, a slice of my white cake with its light, fluffy texture melts in the mouth. At a recent meeting I attended I made the mistake of bringing along a dozen cupcakes as a friendly gesture. After each participant had their cake, business was disrupted as longing eyes were drawn to the last remaining one on the plate. The chairman noticed the problem and devoured the distraction.

When folks ask me for the recipe, I encourage them to carry along an empty travel bag on their next trip to America so they can fill it with '*Betty Crocker Super Moist White Cake Mix*'. While the '*Betty Crocker Creamy Style Vanilla Flavour Ready to Spread Frosting*' I also use is readily available at most Tesco stores, along with the *Super Moist Devil's Food* and the *Super Moist Carrot Cake*, alas, there is no *White*. Now I also have very fine cake recipes that I prepare from scratch when so motivated, but this cake gets so many raves that, when American friends ask me if there is anything I need from the States, I ask for *Betty Crocker White*.

What makes this cake so tasty? Is it the less than 2% of artificial flavour, polyglycerol esters, the propylene glycol monoesters or the xanthum gum? The frosting must surely owe its smooth satisfaction to the sodium stearoyl-2-lactylate E472 (e), the tartrazine, sunset yellow FCF and the

disodium dihydrogen diposphate (E450a). Given this chemical soup, why does everyone rave about this cake?

Perhaps it's because most British cakes I've tried have either one of two consistencies: they are so dry and crumbly you could play that game 'Who can whistle first after a mouthful of British sponge'; or they are so heavy you can use them as doorstops or X-ray shields. How could people who bake such gobsmacking good breads with kinky names like 'bloomers' produce such cake disasters, often with all the flavour of beach sand? And the preoccupation with fondant icing is just as baffling. Now, I know the smooth, rollable stuff looks lovely surrounding a ribbon-tied cake expertly decorated with flowers, the bride and groom or The Lion King. But put a knife to it and it becomes a crumbly mess. And the fondant taste is so cloyingly sweet that even an indiscriminate, compulsive eater like myself needs to run for the coffee or lemonade. Is that why nobody eats the cake at the party but takes it home with them in a paper napkin?

About coffee.

'Brewed?' a waitress once asked me.

'Well, sure. What other kind have you got?' I asked, bewildered.

'Why, some people prefer instant.'

'Oh,' I said.

I wanted to say, 'Why would anyone expect instant coffee from a restaurant? That's something you have in the waiting area of the tyre store.'

And then it happened in my own home. A new friend stopped by.

'Coffee?' I asked.

'Fine,' said she.

As I prepared the coffee maker, she said, 'Oh, no! I can't drink that. It's too strong for me. I only drink instant.'

Since I don't usually keep instant in the house, she settled for tea.

Is instant coffee milder than ground roast? I never heard of that concept before. Doesn't it depend upon how much you use? Even so, where's the taste, the aroma, the romance? Would Meryl Streep wake up in a tent with Robert Redford in the middle of Africa after a tempestuous night expecting *instant* coffee? I don't think so. What's good enough for Meryl is good enough for me.

November '97

Salad Bar None

Since I spent a considerable amount of time last month poking fun at your cakes, I thought I'd make it up to you by sharing a recipe for one of the most crowd-pleasing salads I've had the pleasure of serving. With the holidays approaching and time at a premium, this salad is easy to prepare with all the colours of Christmas.

A little background first. It took me a while to realise that 'salad' in Britain usually means some lettuce leaves, a little watercress, a slice of tomato with a quarter of a radish and a piece of green onion accompanied by 'salad cream', the equivalent in America often known by the brand name 'Miracle Whip', as in 'It's a miracle anyone would eat it'. In the States, especially California, salads are an event. The salad bar is a common fixture at many restaurants with the all-you-can-eat soup and salad buffet a popular combo. Americans love all-you-can-eat anything, which is why we *wear* our food so well, to the disgust of the rest of the world that gives a hoot except Samoa.

But, oh, the places you go at the salad bar! Who needs lettuce? Mounded in oversized bowls sometimes labelled 'fat free', you'll find leafy spinach, raw broccoli, miniature corn cobs and cauliflower, three-bean salads, Chinese chicken salad with crispy ramen noodles, Thai peanut cabbage salad, at least three varieties of potato salad (including a creamy curry), Caesar Salad with or without chicken, a few pasta salads, and shredded carrot salad with raisins. Top up your concoction with diced onions, cherry tomatoes, pickled beets, chopped eggs, cold kernel corn or peas, cubed

ham and bacon and several types of croutons. Grab your own avocado and cover anything not already coated with salad dressing with creamy Italian, honey mustard, blue cheese, yoghurt dill, or thousand island, some of these also marked 'fat free'.

If that doesn't bust a button, do not pass go or collect $200, but go directly to the fruit and dessert bar. Find chocolate custard, tapioca, apple brown betty (apple crumble), whipped cream, fresh strawberries, mounds of melon, whole oranges and apples, soft frozen yoghurt with your choice of toppings like M & Ms or chopped Snickers bars and a partridge in a pear tree.

All this priced for gastronomic excess at $5.95 for lunch and $9.95 for dinner (last time I noticed).

COLOURFUL HOLIDAY SALAD

1 large head cauliflower and 1 large bunch broccoli, uncooked, separated and cut into small bite-sized pieces
1 bunch green onions, chopped
10 slices streaky bacon, fried slowly to cook uniformly crisp (crisp is essential), then broken into small pieces
A handful of raisins
½ cup pine nuts, toasted (other nuts can be used, but I like these best)
1 dozen cherry tomatoes

300 ml mayonnaise
75 ml vinegar (raspberry vinegar adds a nice flavour)
2 to 4 oz. sugar depending on your taste
salt and pepper to taste

Mix together the dressing ingredients, add to and toss with the rest except the cherry tomatoes. Place the mixture in a pretty serving bowl and arrange the tomatoes attractively on top. My recipe says to chill several hours before serving, but I like it at room temperature when the bacon and nuts stay crisp. You can omit the raisins and/or nuts, but the salad loses its pizzazz.

All my sons will be with us in England for Christmas this year, my 21-year-old for the first time. Time to start making those Christmas crackers! Thank you for your kindness this past year, and bless you all this holiday season.

December '97

Traffic School

You're on your way to work on a beautiful California morning. Picture your route to work as an eight-lane version of Silbury Boulevard in Milton Keynes, rather than four. You need to drive about seven miles on this road to get to work and you can see you are going to be stuck in the queue behind the next set of lights for at least three changes. Wild 107.7 Radio entertains you as you sip your Java Express double decaf cappuccino, but you're still annoyed at the traffic. As the third light change advances you forward, you know it's going to be close. As the yellow light glows, you urge the cars in front of you to speed it up. They do and you pass through the intersection as the light is fully red. An irate driver in the cross street honks at you, but you triumphantly progress until your rear view mirror reflects the flashing trio of red, white and blue lights attached to a black and white police car. You rue your hollow victory. Where the #@%* did he come from?

Unless you are really rude to the police officer, this would be considered a minor moving violation. Other minor transgressions might include not fully stopping at a stop sign, making an illegal turn, failing to signal, blocking a pedestrian crossing or exceeding the speed limit by less than 25 miles per hour. Your fate is sealed at the discretion of the public servant facing you.

This time, you get a ticket. Your offence is not serious enough to merit a court appearance. You will pay a hefty fine, but can avoid the possible insurance consequences of careless driver points on your licence if you opt for – TRAFFIC SCHOOL! Yes, traffic school! An eight-hour Saturday session or two four-hour evening sessions spent exploring the Highway Code can keep your DMV (Department of Motor Vehicles) record clean. But chronically unsafe drivers with spare cash cannot use traffic school as a way of avoiding sanctions, as you can attend only once in an 18-month period.

My UK driving instructor informed me of a similar scheme recently introduced in Northampton, an 11-hour course to the tune of £130. Doesn't seem very cost-effective to me. The California county classes cost about $30.

But the state of California has found a way to avoid the costs of administering *all* the traffic school programs to its errant drivers by licensing private traffic schools. The state makes money and you get extra options in carrying out your traffic school sentence. Some schools are staffed by retired police – 'GET YOUR TRAFFIC SCHOOL FROM THE EXPERTS' – a Yellow Pages ad might proclaim. But leave it to American ingenuity to find an opportunity for profit. The following ads for traffic school staffed by stand-up comedians can also be found in my local telephone book:

Comedy for Less
Interactive Seminars *Learn With Humor* Fun Films

Great Comedy School
Cheers! Have Fun with Us & Learn 2

Improv Traffic School
Laughs Galore – You Won't Snore

Lettuce Make You Laugh
(You Get Lunch Too)

Pizza For You – Comedians 2
(For the Pizza Lover)

I Can't Believe I Got a Ticket

Tutors have to cover all the required material in the event an undercover state inspector might intrude. But as a two-time veteran of traffic school and, having first gone the standard route, I'd opt for the comics every time.

February '98

A Yank En Route to LA

My 18-year-old began his university studies last autumn 40 miles east of Los Angeles. Airline price wars and half-term break afforded us the chance to join the 'Family Weekend' activities at his school. Designed to reassure parents that the massive costs of higher education are justified, these weekends are sometimes held at the start of the school year, sometimes at the end and sometimes in the middle like ours. Parents can attend classes, schmooze with the faculty and the university president, sample the cuisine and be encouraged by the Career Centre that – Yes, your child *will* get a job after graduation!

Leaving my husband behind due to an unavoidable business meeting, the other boys and I set off on February 12th.

The Flight

Scheduled departure: 12.00 midday. Actual departure: 1.00 p.m. The captain explains that the delay is caused by a computer crash that requires the cabin crew to do a manual count of passengers on board. Our 747 is only two-thirds full and, with 240 fingers and toes amongst them, wouldn't you think the dozen-strong crew could count faster than that? ... Mealtime at 35,000 feet. You can easily tell who the British children are. They are the ones eagerly consuming the soggy baked beans and chips entrée featured in the kids' meal, while the others are running up and down the aisles begging for extra bread ... Lone mum travelling with Attila the Toddler. Tiring quickly of the Lion King on his

mini-screen, Attila maximises his mother's good fortune in obtaining an entire row to herself by standing on her shoulders and leaping from seat to seat. Occasionally losing his footing, he terrorises the couple in the preceding row by grabbing a bit of hair, ear or headphone in an attempt to restore his balance. Kindly folks who remember their own days cruising with toddlers, they turn, smile sympathetically at mum and sink lower in their seats. Mum exhausts the contents of the Virgin kiddie bag as well as her own supply of diversions within two hours of the 11-hour flight, and our little one cooperates by falling asleep during the last 20 minutes. This mum's resiliency enthrals us as she disembarks with wobbly lad on her shoulders, steadying her son with one hand as she carries her portable pushchair with the other. It must be the bulging backpack on her shoulders that centres her.

Welcome to LA

Behind the wheel of my hired car at 5.00 p.m., LA time, I am reminded of the formidable task of getting from point A to point B in LA. Ribbons of eight to 12-lane freeways merge and bisect each other, and it takes me two hours to complete a trip that should take 50 minutes if I could reach the speed limit. Why would anyone want to live here, I think. Then, as I observe the ocean of colour in the sunset of my rear view mirror, and gaze at the surrounding San Gabriel mountains with their pockets of foothill Americana, I soften. The promises of sunshine, wide open spaces and possible stardom have drawn 30 million strong to prospects of a better life. Since we travellers are three and are deserving of a few brief moments in the short-distanced carpool lane, I wonder how many of the single drivers are hoping the city gates will close soon . . . Off to the Cinema to see *Titanic*. We have a choice between two theatres separated by a giant car park. No problem getting a ticket since there are 30 screens in one theatre and 22 in the other. We opt for the one with a screen the size of the ship. What a voyage! But the best part for me was watching two very overweight American women ask for a large box to spread out their giant-sized servings of popcorn. I wondered why until I saw them piling on the butter at the self-service butter machine. My mouth must have been gaping, for one woman turned to me with a big smile. 'No kernel left uncoated, ya know,' she said. Far from being disgusted, I felt a growing sense of admiration as they so openly flaunted their excess. For as a big lady who can pack it away with the biggest of them, I've only had the nerve to eat like that in private. Just as I am bewildered by those people who only eat because they have to, I am just as amazed at those who overeat without shame or remorse.

February '98

To Market! To Market!

On Wednesdays in the US, most supermarket chains advertise their new specials for the upcoming weekend of shopping. After my recent visit, I took a local San Francisco supermarket newspaper insert and brought it to a Milton Keynes superstore for a comparison. In my conservative conversion rate, $1.60 = £1. The results are shocking, especially since a lot of this is VAT exempt. Could the price of petrol here be partially responsible for the high cost of retail items? I paid $1.09 per gallon (4.4 litres) for gasoline back home. That's 25 cents or 15p per litre.

I am no economist, so I offer no further analysis. Draw your own conclusions.

ITEM	USA MARKET		UK SUPERSTORE	
	$	£	$	£
ROMA TOMATOES (LB)	.69	.43	1.88	1.18
GREEN PEPPERS (LB)	.99	.61	1.74	1.09
RED/GREEN GRAPES (LB)	1.79	1.11	2.06	1.29
CARROTS (LB)	.39	.24	1.20	.75
CAULIFLOWER (LB)	.49	.31	.94	.59
CUCUMBERS (EA)	*1.59*	.99	*1.04*	.65
RED DELICIOUS APPLES (LB)	.89	.56	.94	.59
10 LBS BAKING POTATOES	.99	.61	1.58	.99
NAVEL ORANGES (LB)	*.79*	*.49*	*.75*	*.47*
RED GRAPEFRUIT (3 CT.)	.99	.62	1.87	1.17

ITEM	USA MARKET		UK SUPERSTORE	
	$	£	$	£
GREEN SALAD (BAGS) EA	1.99	1.24	2.22	1.39
MINCE (LB)	*1.79*	*1.11*	*1.58*	*.99*
PORK LOIN CHOPS (LB)	1.99	1.24	4.02	2.52
SILVERSIDE ROAST (LB)	1.99	1.24	5.01	3.13
COOKED PRAWNS (LB)	3.99	2.49	11.62	7.27
CHEDDAR CHEESE (LB)	*4.99*	*3.11*	*2.86*	*1.79*
4 LBS CHICKEN THIGHS	3.50	2.18	6.37	3.98
DORITOS (396 G)	1.99	1.24	3.58	2.24
PARMESAN CHEESE (224 G)	2.99	1.86	4.46	2.79
SAFEWAY WHITE BREAD	.99	.61	.94	.59
15 PACK COKE	3.75	2.34	7.18	4.49
24 PACK BUDWEISER*	10.99	6.86	35.96	22.48
FREIXENET BRUT (75 CL)*	6.49	4.05	11.02	6.89
BOMBAY GIN (75 CL)*	13.99	8.74	20.78	12.99
PEDIGREE CHUM DRY DOG FOOD (10 KILOS)	8.99	5.61	24.60	15.38
3 ROLL PACK KITCHEN ROLL*	1.69	1.05	3.98	2.49
4 ROLL PACK TOILET ROLL*	1.49	.93	3.15	1.97
ALWAYS MAXI 16-24 COUNT*	2.89	1.80	3.18	1.99
TAMPAX 16 COUNT*	2.24	1.40	2.96	1.85
SUBTOTAL	88.33	55.07	169.47	105.99
TAX ON CERTAIN * ITEMS 8.2%	3.26	2.03	–	–
TOTAL	91.59	57.10	169.47	105.99

SPECIAL NOTES: Safeway's own brand of lager 24 count costs £15.49 or $24.78.
2 Litre Pepsi costs $1.29 in the US, Safeway's UK brand costs 95p or $1.52.
bold faced entries reflect cheaper prices in the UK.
I converted measurements and adjusted units when applicable. For example, I only found the 5 kilo size of dog food in the UK superstore, so I doubled the price accordingly.

April '98

Food for Thought

When I was a child, I always hated the word 'humility'. The priests and nuns at school loved to remind us that God appreciated the humble child as they slammed someone's head against a chalkboard or humi*liated* some child whose crime was no more serious than getting a wrong answer or asking a wrong question. I grew into an angry young adult disillusioned not only with the Church, but with the US military/industrial complex, media manipulation and Mom and Apple Pie. I'm still cynical about those things, but not so angry anymore. I've been humbled.

It has been my strange relationship with food that has brought me the most insight into the rest of my imperfections. My battles with fat and food not so coincidentally began as I stood high on the pulpit of self-righteous indignation at society's evils. In the beginning, I dealt with the problem symptomatically by conducting the search for the right diet and experienced what a lot of compulsive eaters do – weight loss followed by weight gain; new diet with more weight loss followed by a greater weight gain. Then I found a support group, a fellowship of people who suggested that my problems with food might need a spiritual solution. Still reeling from memories of Sister David dragging me around the classroom by my ear for the sin of asking for change from a school store purchase, I was in no mood for God. But I felt bad enough about myself that I returned again and again to these pleasant people who suggested that the path to serenity involved taking that finger I was pointing at everyone else and directing it at

myself. I would find my own definition of a spiritual life in the process.

I was asked to list all the people and ideologies I hated, uncover the hurt underneath and then see how the very traits I despised were part of my own makeup. Then I had to see if I was willing to let go of this negativity enough to make a list of all the people I could remember damaging by narrow-mindedness, disregard or direct intention. Then I was to try and find them and make amends. It took me years of work, while kicking and screaming all the way, not because my list was so long, but because I resisted: 'Whaddya mean, I have to take responsibility? I'M the victim here!' I continued to lose and gain hundreds of pounds while I heard testimonials of others about how their lives had changed as a result of honest self-appraisal. Finally, after ten years of struggle, therapy, in-house eating disorder treatment and a variety of eating plans coupled with regular exercise, I began to experience some freedom from the food compulsion, a freedom that lasted more than five years. As I apologised to family, friends, even a former employer to whom I made some financial restitution, the weight of my anger at others lifted, along with the physical weight on my body. I had joined the human race and learned that the best definition of humility was the ability of a person to accept the fact he or she is not God.

I thought I had become one of those folks medical people single out – those 5% of compulsive eaters who remain thin for more than five years. Some of you who have seen me might ask 'What happened? You sure look like you're still having big-time troubles with food.' Damned if I know! Complacency? Lack of faith? I continue to search my soul, trying to understand this strange lack of motivation to be fit again. Maybe I'm afraid of failure *again*, or wary of the intense work I was required to do to stay thin before. I have a good friend who has known me for 28 years. One day she said to me, 'Linda, you have struggled with this weight thing for all your adult life. Give it a rest already. You're a good person. You try to live an honest and ethical life. Why don't you accept yourself and be the best, most attractive fat lady you can be? You're not an axe murderer, for God's sake!'

There are days when I feel so ashamed about this part of my life that I hide out. There are days when I live as my friend suggests and accept the fact that this particular part of me is just one thread in the tapestry of what I often see as a rich weaving of love and good fortune – that God uses this defect of mine to level me when I need it. There are days when I feel certain that at some point I will have had enough physical and emotional pain as a compulsive eater to give it up. Whatever lies in my future, my battles with food continue to create in me a compassion for my fellow human beings as they struggle with their own demons. A compassion I never had in those days when I knew it all.

I was driving home from Towcester a couple of weeks ago, noticing that my automatic transmission was acting up, and finding myself behind a long lorry creeping along. My rational self encouraged patience – all good things come to those who wait. But I was annoyed. Forget the faulty gearbox and go for it! The painted broken road markings give you permission! You've got enough room! So I did what I have often lambasted other drivers for – made a passing move in a possibly dangerous situation. My adrenalin surged as my engine didn't. I slipped back into my proper lane just in time to avoid disaster, sobered and grateful to have another chance to practise what I preach. It might be a long time before I write about the A5 again.

May '98

My Top 25 Reasons for Wanting to Stay Here Forever (at least for now)

In no particular order:
1. My mechanic collects my car for service in the morning and returns it in the evening. He also calls me 'Luvvie' and 'Pet'. I would have hated those names in my serious 20s, but in my philosophical 40s, I'll take all the endearments I can get.
2. I share the road with horses and get that friendly little wave or serious nod (from the rider, not the horse) when I slow down to pass them. I can also drive on the sidewalk sometimes in Stony Stratford.
3. Cream teas (when the scones are warm from the oven and served with clotted cream).
4. The Wakefield Farm Shop. I'm never at a shortage of genuine-made-in-England trinkets for eager friends in the States. Chef makes a mean 'tomahto' soup!
5. When I send a letter it's Royal Mail!
6. *Woods of Windsor* and *Crabtree and Evelyn*. I can pamper myself at a reasonable price.
7. Having Blenheim, Cotswolds, The Royal Theatre in Northampton, Stratford-on-Avon all at a stone's throw (that's American stones; British stones fall closer to home). My home is a threshold to London and the Continent.
8. Your children have given me celebrity status as a storyteller. How many of you have been asked for your autograph on the playground?

9. A sense of belonging to the community. If, as age takes its toll on my health, I am still around these parts, it is comforting to know there is a Forget-Me-Not group of angels on earth.
10. The deer and peacocks sometimes get close enough to call for me at my window.
11. Fabulous cheeses!
12. The ironmonger tells me I'm brilliant when I sign my name on the Switch receipt.
13. Thatched-roofed cottages and English country gardens. (The real thing, not postcards!)
14. If someone writes me a letter, it might close with 'I remain, your ever obedient servant...' Or 'Faithfully Yours.' Such loyalty from a bill collector or insurance broker!
15. Street signs like 'Change of Priorities Ahead'. How do they know so easily what I need? I saw another one just today – 'Clean Hardcore Wanted'. The word 'hardcore' in the US most commonly relates to pornography. I'd like to meet the soul that wants it clean!
16. Hosts go right to your car with you as you leave after an evening in their home and wave to you until you're out of the drive. A little embarrassing when you have to reverse several times to get out of a narrow space.
17. Pre-booking your reserved seating at the cinemas eliminates having to sit through all those trailers. In the States, you better queue up early to get a good seat.
18. Lemon Squash mix with real lemon juice.
19. The prospect of tax-free lottery winnings given all at once. If you win $10,000,000 in the California lottery, you'd get the tax taken out and the money parcelled out over a number of years. Not that I'd complain, if I won the jackpot lottery. I like the scratch cards better – at least I usually break even.
20. People have less of an expectation of being treated nicely. It makes it more fun to do a good turn. Whenever I tip a waitress, she really appreciates it.
21. In the States one party president can do battle with the

other party majority Congress. In the UK, while a party leader is important, you are actually voting for an ideology in your national elections, rather than an individual. So the majority always has control of Parliament until the next election is called. Winners and losers both get to be mocked by Rory Bremner!
22. The Potterspury Village Shop. I can't believe so much merchandise is available in so little space.
23. A six-year-old boy who kisses his girlfriend at school won't get suspended for sexual harassment.
24. People really do say 'Jolly good!'
25. My favourite flower has such a cute name here – 'Busy Lizzy'.

It's hard to believe that I've been writing these essays for nearly three years now, and I'm wondering if you all have had enough of this Yank. Most of the feedback I get from people in the shops has been positive. But I would like to hear from more of you. I've left a 'The Yank Wants to Know' box at the Potterspury Village Shop. Anonymous comments will be accepted, as well as those which are identifiable. If you enjoy my commentaries, let me know what interests you if I haven't covered it already. If you think this column has outlived its usefulness, tell me about it. If you've never liked it, please be gentle!

June '98

L.S.M.F.T.

If I had hoped to receive a mandate to continue this 'Yank' series in response to my query of last month, those hopes have been dashed. Potterspury editor Mags Fenn received one encouraging letter, while I received one positive phone call and one emphatic 'NO' scrawled on the back of a village shop receipt tossed into my 'Yank Wants to Know' box.

I conclude from this paucity of responses that:
1. Very few *Old Mail* recipients actually read my column and I have totally exaggerated my own importance.
2. People might read it but are either too busy or don't think it's worth the time to comment on it.
3. 'It's the old British apathy', as one person suggested. 'If they really wanted you to quit, you would have known by now.'

Since my ego is sufficiently large to convince me that I still have something worthwhile to say, I'll continue writing until I start receiving obscene phone calls and, just to spice things up, share with you a piece I submitted to a storytellers' forum on the Internet. Storytellers are always looking for funny stories for adult audiences, especially as fillers for commentary between longer stories. So, I forewarn you! Stop reading here if your sensibilities are easily offended.

Back in the 50s and early 60s when cigarette advertising was in its heyday, there was a brand of US cigarette known as Lucky Strike. Lucky's long lasting ad campaign contained an anagram for a slogan: L.S.M.F.T. – Lucky Strike Means Fine Tobacco. Some members of the general population

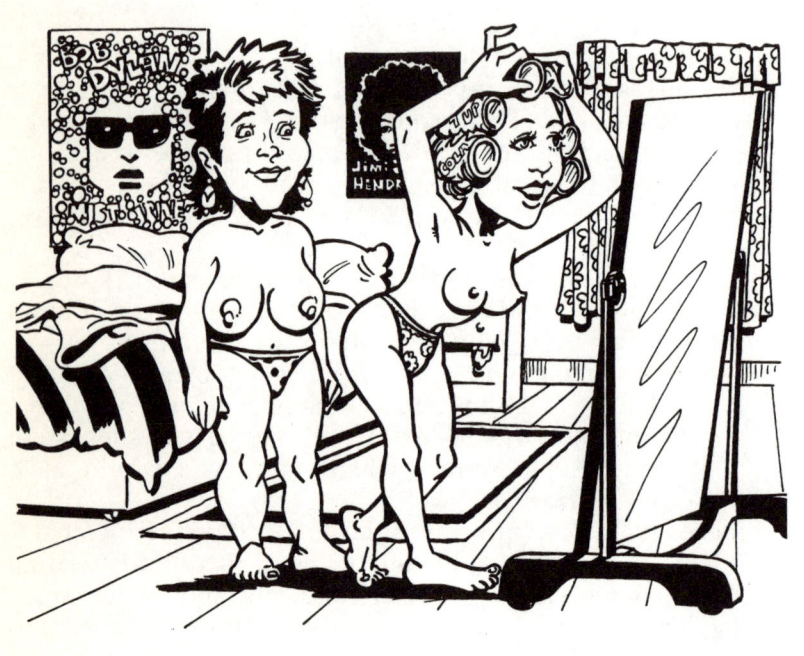

had other ideas. On the playgrounds of New York, you could often hear 'Loose Straps Mean Floppy Tits'.

At the ripe old age of 13, I had a friend who thought it expedient to warn me I was 'low-breasted', a liability which might cause me a problem in later life. She was right because my whole life has been spent trying to find just the right bra to call my appendages to attention without leaving permanent grooves in my shoulders. Indeed, I have always had breasts of the floppy variety right from their first little buddings.

It was my misfortune to experience young adulthood during the 'burn your bra' days, which spawned debate over which breasts were suitable for such loose living. There was a test one could do. Put a pencil under a breast and if it could hold the pencil, you were too floppy. Well, since mine could hold a can of baked beans and more resembled eggplants (aubergines) than melons, I decided not to offend the human landscape by untethering mine. This was at a time when I was still thin.

I remember when I first left home in 1969 to share a flat with some girls I didn't know. Rather a naive 18-year-old and a product of twelve years of Catholic school, I was amazed to meet my new, just-turned-16-year-old roommate who had told the high school principal to take his school and shove it. (In the States, you must complete four years of secondary school in order to graduate. She had only finished two.) She had just entered the work force by lying through her teeth about her age and qualifications. A dear friend now for nearly 30 years, she had the boobs of the stand-up variety which caused me no end of fascination as she never wore a bra. She'd come home from work complaining about her 'shmaggeggy' boss and stomp up and down the hallway of our NY railroad flat, called 'railroad' because the narrow rooms were built one behind the other. I'd find myself staring at her lovely adornments as they swayed gently and provocatively under her clothing. Of course, she hated her long, natural curly hair and spent much time at the ironing board pressing out the curls, then rolling her hair in fizzy drink cans for a gentle wave. It helped about as much as my breast harnesses, but at least I knew she had trouble with her self-image as well.

Our future lives called us to different parts of the USA, but when I saw her again after about fifteen years, she still was braless with no L.S.M.F.T. problems that I could discern. While we relaxed in the skinny in the outdoor jacuzzi on a beautiful California night, I finally got the courage to ask her if I could touch her amazing breasts. (By this time I was a mother of three who had nursed all her kids for a couple years each, so fuggedabout what mine were like! The only benefit from all that nursing was that my breasts had been good for something and I was left with permanently extended nipples. I'm convinced that my breasts are the inspiration for the current 'Everybody needs a bosom for a pillow' song). Pat loved her boobs, so she was more than happy to share them with me. I shyly reached out my hands and gave them a little squeeze.

Shazayam! They felt just like the fake ones health practitioners show to women for breast self-examination – the ones that they put a little lump in so you know what that would feel like. Only hers had no lump, just a nice squishy feel. I saw her again last year and, wouldn't you know it, at the age of 44, Patricia still goes braless. Still no sign of L.S.M.F.T! More astounding to me than the World Trade Center's twin towers in New York City.

I once was in a workshop for women on sex. You know what I'm talking about. The kind where we get to take risks and share our innermost fears and longings. I really wanted to find out the true definition of multiorgasms – a phenomenon that women are supposedly so lucky to experience. Was that more than one in one minute or five minutes, an hour, a month, I wanted to know? I'm still not sure! The group leader was a genial woman in her forties describing her own sexual life. When she said, 'You know how some women have breasts that are 36A, 38B or 34C? Well, mine are 36 Longs,' I knew I had found a kindred spirit!

I'll close with another anagram that, if recognised by you,

will give away your age as easily as the pouches under your eyes – S.W.A.L.C.A.K.W.S. It was often placed on the back of the envelope in a young girl's correspondence. I'll reveal the meaning next month.

July–August '98

Transatlantic Confusion

In my youthful fantasies of love and marriage, I assumed I would live in one place with the man of my dreams, have some kids and watch them and their friends mature into adults while our friends did the same. It was not to be. My husband's career has moved us six times in 24 years – from Dallas, Texas, to Indianapolis, Indiana; on to Boston, Massachusetts, then to Atlanta, Georgia. From Atlanta it was on to San Francisco, where we remained for nine years before our transfer to England.

When the children started coming, our moves became traumatic for me as I invariably became a part of the new community we inhabited, and when a new move was imminent, the thought of making a new home and new friends in a strange place overwhelmed me. I was sure that I would never find friends as wonderful as the ones I was leaving. Jack never felt these anxieties as his identity usually revolved around work, and since each move enhanced his career, he moved on in eager anticipation of the new challenges he would face. He would begin work in the new location while I handled the intricacies of the moves themselves. I shed many tears as I placed my memories in our moving boxes. Each time we were uprooted, I would tell Jack that this would be the last move I would make.

I learnt early on that to make friends I needed to be a friend. I learnt not to wait for the neighbours to knock on my door with a warm welcome and a hot apple pie. I learnt to knock first and extend that invitation for coffee. If I met a young mum with her kids in the park and, after a chat, took a liking to her, I'd ask her over. Even if I feared rejection, I'd act as if I had something to offer and do it anyway. My interests led me to befriend people of various dispositions, ages and sizes. On a rare occasion, a friend would have a spouse or child who attracted my whole family into friendship.

I have been fortunate enough to find in each place I've lived one or two friends who become the soft pillows I sink into from time to time, who see the good in me when I only feel shame, who give me a kick in the butt when deserved and who enjoy singing and dancing to the oldies on a friends' night out. While knowing them has changed me irrevocably and their bit of divinity is part of my soul, it is the absence of their daily presence that I mourn with each move.

I've discovered that it takes about three years for me to recover from the loss of a familiar home to adapt to a new one. It is usually in the third year's return visit to a former neighbourhood or town that I find that the longings for the old familiarities have lessened.

The third year of my UK adventure has come and gone. I sit here in Maryland at my sister's computer during the fourth week of my annual USA visit and, while I am grateful for the precious time with her and her family, I feel disoriented. 'Where's home? Where do I belong?'

These questions first came to mind as I headed towards my California house in mid-July. I looked at the unique San Francisco landscape with the summer fog rolling in, surfed the car radio for a familiar tune, was dazzled by the blue sky and felt totally out of place. Had enough time elapsed in England for me to be looking at my homeland with the eyes of a foreigner? The sight of oversized cars quickly burning their supplies of 12p a litre fuel, the endless stream of stores and restaurants (do we really need one McDonald's per mile?), the luxury of backyard swimming pools, the enormous energy draw of thousands of air-conditioners keeping us ever so comfortable as the

mercury hits 105, created in me a sense of wonder at the tremendous wealth the United States possesses. I never noticed it so much before. I don't think most Americans do. I felt guilty.

When I got to my home town, I didn't get to spend much time with my best buddies right away, since their lives were busy with a rhythm of their own. Under the pretence of jet lag, I turned up the air-conditioning enough to feel cold, so I could burrow under the covers and hide. My husband, who doesn't suffer from the weight of Americana on his shoulders, proceeded to enjoy it all – playing golf without getting covered in mud, going to the cinema with our older sons, languishing in his favourite bookstores, devouring bagels and American bacon – and was surely perplexed at my depression. I missed my British friend Shirley and the winds whistling through my house in England.

Then I saw Patricia – the L.S.M.F.T. Patricia. Her delight in seeing me and her enthusiasm for having a few days off from work were infectious. 'Linda, you're the only one I know who could be by a swimming pool in the beautiful California sunshine and feel guilty about it.' I told her about the article I wrote extolling the virtues of her anatomy. She blushed and gushed, 'With all you know about my life and times, *you chose to focus on my tits?*' As I enjoyed my time with the guileless Patricia, the ribald Valerie, Earth Mother Julienne, always-giving Mary and soul-searching Scott, as well as delighting in my husband's happy face as the pressures of work were lifted from him for a time, I realised that my riches and security have always come from those I love and those who love me.

For now, England is my home. When the time comes for me to leave, I'm sure it will be just as traumatic as my other moves. But new places have opened up my mind, helped me to appreciate my blessings, appreciate my loving parents and sister. I might wonder where I belong, but when I ask myself which stranger who became a friend I would trade for the physical stability of life in one home and one community, I have no answer.

Notes on 'S.W.A.L.C.A.K.W.S.' – July/August *Old Mail*

Most of you know that 'S.W.A.K.' has often been placed on an envelope to convey that its contents are 'Sealed With A Kiss'. At some unknown time, a nameless upstart altered the standard phrase and we 60s kids used the revised 'Sealed With A Lick 'Cause a Kiss Won't Stick' to show we were really cool.

September '98

Clinton's Calamity

'So, what do you think about Clinton?'

Whether I am buying apples or stamps or having a phone conversation with an acquaintance, my American accent must be inspiring the frequency with which I have been asked this question in the last few days. Of course, the fact that your press is devoting a disproportionate amount of ink to the subject (14 pages out of the first 32 in the September 12th issue of the *Times*), may have something to do with it as well. And since most British folks mispronounce my surname by calling me 'Lewinsky', they must think I have an inside scoop on the affair.

I have long stopped believing that American presidents are anything close to being statesmen. To reach that elevated position of power, one has to have promised too many things to too many people along the way to maintain personal integrity. The only president in my lifetime whom I would even consider coming close to honourable was the one most political analysts consider one of the biggest failures – Jimmy Carter. I remember how he was ridiculed as a country bumpkin by admitting in a magazine interview that he 'had lusted in my heart' after women other than his wife. How far we've come!

It's not the details of Clinton's sexual escapades in the Oval Office that shock or embarrass me. My husband informed me many years ago that most men would find a hole in the wall an adequate sexual partner if the time were right. And how many of us would be devastated if skeletons in our own sexual closets were revealed? That Clinton should find a handy playmate in a ripe, young White House intern who was infatuated with him hardly surprises me. And, while the morality and ethics of cheating on your wife in the workplace where loyal employees can be compromised may be reprehensible to me personally, that is not what disgusts, angers and amazes me the most. The combination of arrogance and stupidity that, in this climate of politics by character assassination, caused him to think he wouldn't get caught, is what blows me away. And that, when he got caught, he assumed he could lie his way out of it. This, despite continuous media intrusion into his sexual affairs since 1992.

Could he not see that any hint of further impropriety could bring down his presidency as the conservative, religious right relentlessly pursued him? Could he actually think he had any personal privacy? Could anyone in his right mind rationalise that fellatio was not included in the dictionary of sexual behaviours? What about the advisors he chose to surround himself with? Did no one ever say to him, 'Look, Bill. If you've got to get it on, here are a few smutty magazines. Get thee to the bathroom and take care of yourself! But don't embarrass us, yourself, your wife, your daughter and your country by getting caught in another compromising position. Don't the names Jennifer Flowers or Paula Jones ring a bell?'

When his affair with Monica Lewinsky was made public back in January, he could have realised the jig was up. If I had been his spin doctor, I would have suggested the following speech which would at least have given the hint of honesty and remorse so appreciated by the average person when a wrongdoing has been discovered. Even better if actually heartfelt:

My fellow Americans,
I am a flawed man. As much as I love this country and have pursued a political career to bring about changes needed to bring peace and prosperity to every man, woman and child in America, I have let you down.

My inability to live up to my own moral standards when it has come to women has been a weakness that has threatened for years to destroy my marriage, my family and my job. I don't know why my wife puts up with me. I am grateful beyond measure for her love and loyalty.

I cannot try to cover my tracks any longer. Allegations about sexual improprieties with both Paula Jones and Monica Lewinsky are unfortunately true. I have misused the power given to me as a public servant in a quest for sexual gratification and I am ashamed. I have instructed my lawyers to offer a reasonable settlement to Ms. Jones and I apologise. both to her and Ms. Lewinsky for subjecting them to public ridicule. While I question the motives of Special Prosecutor Starr in pursuing me in this manner, I will, nonetheless, cooperate with his investigation and hope he will not trouble Ms. Jones or Ms. Lewinsky further. If to resign would better honour the integrity of this office, I am willing to do so.

But I don't want to leave this office in disgrace. I still have two years in my term. I put myself at the mercy of our system of checks and balances and at the judgment of you, my fellow Americans, to decide my fate. There is nothing I would like better than to continue my work as your public servant. I hope that in time I can redeem myself, not only in your hearts, but in the hearts of those who matter most to me – my wife and daughter.

In the recent film The American President, *the ficticious President Andrew Shephard suffers a campaign of character assassination waged by his political enemies. He tells the American people that the presidency is not just partially based on character, but 'entirely' based on character. If only I had remembered that, I might have saved us all a lot of trouble.*

Thank you.

Well, so much for Fantasyland in politics.

I do believe that Kenneth Starr made a strategic error in quickly releasing his report over the Internet. Supplying the more prurient details of the President's sexual encounters I believe will anger the general population, lending credence to the theory that the Republicans have been out to get him all along. If the Republican Party has hopes that the furore around the Lewinsky affair will bring more Republicans into local government, Congress and, ultimately the White House in the year 2000, they might be surprised at the real outcome. Additionally, the American economy has been in a state of prosperity during the Clinton administration. Americans will not appreciate this upstart rocking the boat over sex when their wallets are fatter.

As embarrassed as I might feel as an American living abroad while this folly unfolds, I was more chagrined when Clinton rejected a complete landmine ban as threatening to American interests in Korea. I was more embarrassed at the recent terrorist-retaliation bombings in Africa and Asia. That this lying excuse for a President and his whole entourage regularly make life and death decisions of worldwide magnitude is not just embarrassing, it is frightening.

September '98

NOTE: The *Old Mail* editor actually did not publish this piece since she felt that this particular piece of commentary might prove offensive to some members of the community. She did publish the following piece, so those of you who read this book version get an extra one! Oh, by the way. Clinton settled with Paula Jones for $850,000 on November 13th.

Doing Business in the UK

Life in the UK annoys me the most when your approach to doing business inconveniences or irritates me. Like the time I went to the video store with some money in my pocket, but having forgotten my wallet. I found the movie of my choice, approached the clerk and explained the situation. Now, my family has rented films from this place nearly every weekend that we have been here, and this woman has seen me many times. But her reply was, 'Sorry, I can't let you have a film without any ID.'

I laughed. 'You're kidding, right? You've seen me a hundred times in this shop. How many fat American ladies by the name of Lewandowski have accounts here?'

'That doesn't matter. Company policy says I must see ID.'

I retreated in a huff, wishing I was at the shop back home where they would have said, 'Oh, that's okay, Mrs. Lewandowski. We trust you.'

But I have to tell you about my latest encounter with BT. I recently received a call from a pleasant young BT representative whose voice indicated puberty was not far behind. He wanted to make sure I was saving as much money as possible with my phone service. To streamline the prose I will avoid using the repetitive 'he said' and 'I said'. The BT man is in boldface type, I am in normal type, and my aside comments are in italics.

'Have I reached the number of Jack Cosgrove?' *(My husband's name. I kept my own name when I married, even if it does belong to my father.)*

'Yes.'

'I'm calling from BT to make sure you are receiving the kinds of services that are saving you the most money. Have you got about 5 minutes to go over your account with me?'

(Reluctantly) 'All right.'

'I see you already have the call minder answering service, but not call waiting where people can get through while you are already on the phone.'

'I don't like to be beeped when I'm in the middle of another conversation. Besides, I have enough trouble carrying on one conversation without trying to carry on two.'

'Lovely. What about caller display where you can see the phone number of the caller before you answer, or call return where you can find out the number of the last person to call you? Or maybe you'd like call diversion where people can speak to you even if you are away from home?'

'Smashing, but I am diverted enough already.'

'Yes, but you can add all of these Select Services for only £11 per quarter.'

'Well, I'm trying to simplify my life. So, I think I'll pass.'

'Brilliant. We do have a special 25% discount service on the number you call most frequently in your Friends and Family scheme. It's only £1 a month.'

'Now, that sounds good. I want you to use my Internet access number. I'm not sure, but I think it's already listed as a Friends and Family number. Can you read off the numbers so I can check?'

'I'm sorry, Madam. *(Uh Oh! He's calling me 'Madam'. A bad sign.)* **I cannot do that since your name is not on the account. That's confidential information.'**

(The hairs on my neck begin to rise) 'Oh, I see. You are telling me that it's all right for me to authorise extra services that will incur additional charges on Jack Cosgrove's account. But I have no authority to ask you for one of the phone numbers that I, his wife, have supplied to you as the person who set up the Friends and Family scheme for this account in the first place.' *(I'm getting really steamed now!)* 'Despite the fact that my signature has appeared on every

cheque you have ever received in payment for this account? IS THIS WHAT YOU ARE TELLING ME???'

(Poor Bloke) **'Well, that appears to be the case.'**

'Well, I'll tell you. It APPEARS that I am going to hang up on you. I rarely hang up on callers such as yourself, because I know you are just doing what you are told. But don't you think this is a strange policy your company has? You don't know me. How would you know I'm not some crazy person out to get Jack Cosgrove by ordering call waiting, call return, call diversion and caller display when he least suspects it? Yet, you'd even encourage this behaviour from someone whose name is not listed on the account.'

'Well, I ah ... Does that mean you don't want the 25% discount?'

(Click)

October '98

My Life as a Storyteller

I am often asked, 'How did you get to be a storyteller?'

When I was a young mum with three little ones, I made the unilateral decision to toss out the television, a detriment to my children's development. My husband went along with the experiment. In the year and a half we were TV-less, we played lots of games, listened to more music, and I read, read, read to my children the countless books we hauled in regularly from the library. It was during one of these reading sessions that a visiting friend excitedly told me of her recent experience of listening to a professional storyteller. After hearing me read to the boys, she was sure I had storytelling talent.

I had done a little drama in high school, enjoyed it thoroughly, but didn't have much self-confidence. Tentatively, I began storytelling by memorising children's books and poems and reciting them to audiences mainly consisting of the pupils in my children's schools. The response from teachers and children was encouraging. I then attended a storytellers' workshop where I heard that the art of storytelling is best communicated from the heart and soul in the teller's own words. I had already begun to see the difficulties in 'reciting' a story. If I flubbed a word or forgot a section, I couldn't easily recover. And when I heard a few other storytellers in performance, I knew I had to begin truly 'telling' my stories if I was to mature in the craft.

My biggest enemy was (and still is) my fear of failure. So, over the next ten years, my efforts were sporadic as I was dogged by depression, embarrassed by my looks and overwhelmed by parental and household responsibilities. The times when I did tell stories, I felt the glow of exhilaration that comes from work one loves.

When I got to England, my number one priority was to help my youngest child adapt to his first school as well as to his new country. The best way to do that, to my mind, was to be at his school as much as possible. Tired of being self-absorbed in Linda-angst, I took a crack at storytelling in earnest, sharing stories at my son's school whenever I had the chance. The more I told, the more confident I felt. The impact of delight, the awe and wonder I saw on the children's faces as their imaginations took flight, the special intimacy a storyteller and her listener share, all had me hooked. I was also taking college classes, trying to find a career niche for the second half of my life, but ultimately decided to concentrate on the stories instead.

I spent most of the 1997–98 school year thrusting myself on surrounding schools in a volunteer capacity as a way of building up a reputation. Volunteers to support the literacy curriculum are few and far between, so I was heartily welcomed by 25 schools in the course of that time. I mostly provided a series of sessions with the children on a once per week basis for several weeks. I would spend a half or whole day with a school and work with the entire school in divided groups. Other storytellers I began to meet told me it was bad for business for me to volunteer my time, that my work had real value and should merit payment. I did not disagree, but I knew that school budgets did not allow for many extras, that I was a new commodity, and that volunteering in the schools gave me added experience as a new 'professional'. The schools were more than happy for me to send a note home to parents during a series describing what I was doing with their children, and encouraging them to continue reading aloud to their kids even after the young ones could read for themselves. Details of 'Stories with Linda' as children's party entertainment were prominently displayed on my letterhead. So while I haven't created much

revenue from my schools work, my party business has consistently grown.

This year I've blitzed the Milton Keynes schools with my promotional materials, including many of the glowing references I have received. My suggested schedule of fees, though modest, has not created the same kind of demand I received last year, even though I emphasised in big block capitals: 'I never refuse to work with a school over money.' Since working on July's Milton Keynes Storytelling Festival, I am beginning to cultivate adult audiences and to move into organising 'DIY' workshops on how folks can develop their own storytelling skills.

My passion for storytelling continues to grow as I peruse my newly acquired volumes of stories in search of new material. The walls in my study are filled with artwork and stories created by children who have been energised by storytelling as an art form that has lain dormant in our world of mechanised entertainment. I have witnessed first-hand the love and gratitude children are so willing to give to someone who they perceive respects them enough to look them in the eye and spend an hour validating their world of imagination and fantasy. I have also had the privilege of watching the adults I've worked with relax, forget about their mortgages, stressful marriages and the state of the state and join that same world of pleasure.

Here's a small anecdote from my experience at Kingsthorpe Lower School in Northampton. I had just finished working with a reception class and was manoeuvring my way to the next class through the cluster of little bodies on the floor, when I heard a tiny voice whisper to his mate: 'Do you think she's a man?'

'I don't know. Do *you* think she's a man?'

Now, I may be a large woman, but I am known for my unusual dresses and jewellery, so this comment took me by surprise. I smiled and turned to wave a goodbye, when the same little voice piped up loudly: 'Do you know Mrs. Doubtfire?'

'No,' I replied with a giggle. 'But if I run into her you'll be the first to know.'

This was not the first time my storytelling delivery had reminded someone of Robin Williams, but to be considered a compatriot of Mrs. Doubtfire? I left that room well-chuffed indeed!

November '98

Volunteering

I've spent a lot of time during my adult life as a volunteer in a variety of capacities. Partly because I've heard that a generous heart lasts longer, partly because it makes me feel good, partly to assuage a deep-seeded feeling of guilt that I don't often deserve to be here on this earth, so I better leave my square of it in better shape than when I found it or begin my next life as a worm (a fat one at that).

As a parent volunteer, I have co-ordinated a variety of fundraising projects on both sides of the Atlantic in support of academic, social and sports programs. I can say unequivocally that it is more difficult obtaining volunteers here both in the planning and implementation phases of a project than it is in the States. I've tried to figure out why. Several thoughts come to mind, though these observations are just that – observations of a foreigner at whom you may just want to scream 'Yankee go home!!'

1. *British folks proceed with greater caution.*
   Sometimes it seems that people lack confidence in their own abilities. Especially when it comes to a leadership role. They fear they will not have the time or organisational skills needed to be successful at the task. If they are women, they fear that their spouses will not provide the extra child care and household support that might be needed for attendance at meetings or time spent on paperwork and telephoning. 'I need to leave the meeting early to get my husband's dinner'; 'I can't get to the meeting because I have to put the children to bed'; 'My

husband gets angry because he says I do too much already or spend too much time on the phone'; these are refrains I've heard women echo too many times to be isolated instances.

You also are more hesitant to ask for things. I was in a ladies' restroom queue in a restaurant once where there was sparse toilet paper in the stalls. The available paper was happily passed on from woman to woman, one woman remarking, 'I never go out without taking my own reserve', but no one went to the manager to ask for more. When a child guilessly asks, 'Can I come over and play today at your house?', he is often admonished for being rude. I've seen people trying to pack their shopping at the till while struggling with squirrelly children; they don't ask for assistance, but if an employee happens to come along, they are grateful. Perhaps it's the old 'stiff upper lip' syndrome. But this tendency inhibits the assertiveness necessary to ask for raffle prizes and volunteers, either by phone or direct contact.

Different perceptions of what constitutes 'a lot of work'.
When we hold school fetes in my California community, it is considered a little job to work on the day of the event. Keep in mind that our school fairs can run all day. If you were responsible for running a game stall, you might be required to find your stall's volunteers and schedule them in advance, get to school early, set up the stall with the equipment provided for you and supervise it for the day, though you wouldn't need to be there constantly. You would answer to the Game Stalls Chairperson who, with her helpers, has the big job. It would be that person's responsibility with his/her committee to decide which games would be played at the fete, to design them and procure the equipment needed to assemble them, map out the area and get the volunteers to run the stalls. Since the average school might need to entertain 500 children plus their parents, there would have to be a large variety of activities to develop. Many

are tried and true crowd-pleasers from the past with bits and pieces stored in a central location from year to year, but there are always some new games offered.

In my village experience, it's often been hard to find people just to work a stall that's already been set up for them. When most of the fetes here last only a couple of hours, it is hard to fathom why someone would consider that a lot of work. 'I don't want to have all my time taken up working a stall. I'll miss the fete' and 'My mother (or other relative) has decided to come to the fete. It would be rude of me to leave her on her own' are reasons I've been given for declining to work a stall. Baked goods stalls sell out within a half-hour and are excellent money makers. Yet at the last two fetes I worked on in England, the coordinator found herself hunting for cakes because people didn't contribute as much. I would see store-bought scones and cookies on the table. You just wouldn't see that at a cake stall in the States, where people would want to bring their best recipes along for sale. A 'Cakewalk' is a favourite game for school fairs there. Players dance to popular music around a numbered maze until the music stops. Then a number is drawn. If you've landed on the drawn number you win a whole cake. Imagine having enough cakes donated for a cake stall with goods for sale, plus the 'Cakewalk' game which usually runs for several hours!

Attending a PTA meeting here once a term is considered a lot of work. Americans don't like meetings either, but a PTA executive committee at a local primary school might consist of 20 people doing a variety of jobs, and part of their job descriptions include regular attendance at the monthly meetings. Besides the officers' jobs of Chair, Vice-Chair, Recording Secretary, Correspondence Secretary and Treasurer, there's often a person called Member-at-Large, who is the former chair who makes herself/himself available to help the new folks on board. We also have a hospitality chair who takes care of organising refreshments at events. There will be a

Coordinator of Volunteers, a Leavers' (Graduates') Party Chair, a Staff Liaison, and Chairs of all the individual events, not all of which raise money, but are designed as spirit boosters. There's probably also a Newsletter editor and a representative to the local education authority. And none of these could function well without each class having a parent representative expected to attend the monthly meetings to feed back information from the parents and to help with the procurement of event volunteers. More than one past committee at my British school has tried the Class Rep idea. People volunteer, then take no initiative and don't want to attend our PTA term meetings.

3. *People spend more time within their family groups.*
Just as your geographical position as an island can create a feeling of isolation from the rest of the European community, I observe that retreat into the safety and predictability of one's own family occupies more of your time than it does that of the average American. Your entire country is about the size of California. Even if you live in the North and your parents are in the South, the need to establish one's self in the greater community is less acute than when you must create an extended family because you've moved across a 3000 mile-wide country. Many people in my California community are not natives to the state and are therefore anxious to become involved so they can make friends.

4. *On some levels, life is more difficult.*
The average person has to work harder here to keep his or her head above water. Wages are low. The cost of food, housing and petrol are high. Unless your job includes a company car, a perk much more prevalent here than in the US, it appears that there is often little incentive for high achievement. Workers don't often feel appreciated. You are grateful for the smallest kindnesses. Sometimes I think you just get plain worn out.

5. *The weather.*
   Long stretches of grey skies, rainy or drizzly days can make anyone want to stay at home with a good book or the telly.

December/January '98

Am I Blushing?

Regular readers of the *Old Mail* are already aware of some incidents in the UK I would rather forget. Like the time I left my purse in plain sight in my teacher's car while we toured a museum and his car was vandalised (March '96). Sadly there are more.

I had been in England for only a short time when I paid my first visit to the Derngate Theatre. I had invited a new friend to come along and we had a stimulating evening watching several young male dancers called the Tap Dogs tap their way across the stage in various states of dress or undress. On the way home, we stopped at the local pub in Paulerspury where the crowd was happy, the conversation noisy. I offered to buy the first round of drinks and placed my order with the bartender while my friend found us a table. Upon receiving the drinks and my change, I left the server a pound tip. 'And what do you want me to do with that?' he said loudly. All other bar conversation ceased as my face reddened while customers turned to focus on me. 'Why, it's a tip for you,' I stammered. 'Well, you don't need to do that around here,' he laughingly replied, and returned my pound to me. All eyes watched the newcomer to Britain as I made a hasty retreat with drinks in hand and eyes lowered as the chuckles followed me. When I related the scene to my waiting friend, she outlined proper pub etiquette – offer to buy the barkeep a drink; tipping is bad form. I have since discovered that it is only bad form if you aim to tip the publican himself. Most of his employees are more than happy to receive an extra pound here or there.

But now I take the direct approach when it comes to tipping bartenders. 'Are you one of those servers who get insulted when someone offers you a tip?', I ask. 99.9% of the time I hear 'No, not me. I'm surely not one of those,' as the palm is extended.

It took me a long time to grasp that the greeting 'Are you all right?' from a Brit is a form of casual hello. When an American greets you in the same way, it's usually because he or she knows you have been having a hard time of late and wonders how you are coping. After a few experiences of people I hardly knew asking me if I was all right, paranoia set in. These British people must be extra perceptive, I thought. I felt like I was in one of those dreams where you are naked and nobody else is. Could they tell I'm a little nervous in this new country? How did they know that I was upset because my oldest son never calls me? Did my depression over my weight show that day? So I started replying like this. 'Well, my husband's angry with me because I lost his favourite pen. I knew I shouldn't have grabbed it in the first place. And I was a little down yesterday because I held up the queue in the market as I fiddled with the new money and the people behind me seemed annoyed. You know how Americans often act like know-it-alls and I don't want to come across as one of *them*. I miss my best friend back home and somebody gave me the finger in the roundabout today because I forgot about lane discipline. And while I was eating lunch, I saw this article in the newspaper about how the orphans in Bosnia are treated, and I just crawled back to bed feeling so ashamed about eating *anything* while those children are starving. But I'm feeling better now.' One day as I stood waiting for my son outside the school fence, I noticed another mum greeting everyone she knew with 'Are you all right?'. Since most replies were either a simple 'Yes' or 'Fine', I figured out why people seemed to be avoiding me.

I was on my first Christmas Fete committee and we were having a planning meeting. My job was to coordinate the raffle. One volunteer said she had obtained some nice prizes. I eagerly gave her my attention as she listed the two swim passes from the local leisure centre, the two free Happy Meals from McDonald's and the £5 gift voucher from a hairdresser. 'Where do you usually go to get the top prizes, you know, like the TVs or bicycles, the weekends at a Bed & Breakfast?' I ventured. I was mortified, as I realised from the looks I received, that those modest donations from local businesses reflected what you would normally expect at an average school raffle. Of course, I didn't know then what I know now. Most people here are happy to win just a little something. Giving 50p or £1 for 5 chances on a £1.99 bottle of wine is a usual practice upon entering an event. Five chances will cost you $5 in an American raffle, so prizes there matter more.

This last one comes from the mouth of babes. My irreverent version of 'Little Rabbit FooFoo', a naughty little bunny who gets in trouble with the Good Fairy, is my most requested story. At one point FooFoo is hiding under his bed as his mother tries to bring him to the waiting GF. I describe in detail the disorder there. I often vary what surrounds FooFoo under his bed, but for a long time referred to the dirty underwear as 'dirty knickers', until one little boy piped up, 'If FooFoo is a boy bunny, what is he doing with dirty knickers under his bed?' I didn't realise that the word 'knickers' is more often applied to girls' underwear.

February '99

Welcome to the United States

It's early morning and the drone of interstate highway traffic near my parents' Florida home fills my head as I rub the sleep from my eyes. Since no bedroom light seeps through the cracks of the adjacent bedroom door as it did on the two previous mornings, I assume that my best British friend and her daughter have finally been relieved of their jet lag and something approaching a good night's sleep has overtaken them.

It's the first trip to America for the two behind the bedroom door. When, months ago, I furiously clipped tokens from the *Daily Mail* to secure half-price airline tickets, I envisioned their delight as the warm Florida sun would warm their bodies and their toes would first grace Gulf of Mexico waters. I longed to give them a taste of real-life America, not just fast food and theme parks. I did not expect that initiation to be had on the airplane itself in the form of the US Immigration & Naturalisation Service (INS) landing card, number I-94W – the one most foreign-born vacationers are required to complete before passing through US customs.

Welcome to the United States headlines the card in boldface type. As I assisted my friends in deciphering the first side of the form, I noticed it resembled its British counterpart. But the opposite side went right for the jugular in the INS attempt to prevent unsavoury characters from blighting the American landscape. I give you questions 'A' through 'G' (tick yes or no) verbatim:

A. Do you have a communicable disease; physical or mental disorder, or are you a drug abuser or addict?
B. Have you ever been arrested or convicted for an offense or crime involving moral turpitude or a violation related to a controlled substance; or been arrested or convicted for two or more offenses for which the aggregate sentence to confinement was five years or more; or been a controlled substance trafficker; or are you seeking entry to engage in criminal or immoral activities?
C. Have you ever been or are you now involved in espionage or sabotage; or in terrorist activities; or genocide; or between 1933 and 1945 were you involved, in any way, in persecutions associated with Nazi Germany or its allies?
D. Are you seeking to work in the U.S.; or have you ever been excluded and deported; or been previously removed from the United States; or procured or attempted to procure a visa or entry into the U.S. by fraud or misrepresentation?
E. Have you ever been detained, retained or withheld custody of a child from a U.S. citizen granted custody of the child?
F. Have you ever been denied a U.S. visa or entry into the U.S. or had a U.S. visa cancelled? If yes, when? _____ where? _____
G. Have you ever asserted immunity from prosecution?

Does the INS really think that actual drug traffickers, child snatchers, Nazi war criminals, terrorists, spies, visa frauds and perpetrators of genocide will answer these questions honestly? I don't think so. Even the INS isn't that stupid. The absurdity continued with an 'Important' admonition: 'If you have answered **"YES"** to any of the above, please contact the American Embassy **BEFORE** you travel to the U.S. since you may be refused admission into the United States.' Great advice at 35,000 feet!

What could possibly be the INS motive for such questions, I angrily thought. As flight attendants retrieved many first-try mistakes from confused passengers and distributed replacement cards freely, I wondered whether it was another instance of warning foreign visitors who's boss. Many Americans couldn't even pronounce 'turpitude', no less define it, I thought. Bill Clinton immediately came to mind.

I wanted to apologise to these tourists who had probably clipped their tokens as religiously as I did to maximise their hard-earned holiday funds for a bit of Mickey Mouse and the American Dream. And to add insult to injury, it is suggested in another part of the form that it should take you six minutes to complete the form – two minutes to learn about the form, four minutes to fill it out. So besides being warned that you better behave from the mountains to the prairies, to the oceans white with foam, you can feel secure in knowing that your intelligence may be below par as well. Of course you can write to the INS in New York to let them know if they have erred in their time estimate.

Many years ago, Teddy Roosevelt coined a phrase describing a sensible course of action for the US government: 'Speak softly and carry a big stick.' Do we ever learn?

March '99

A Story

Mary Margaret was a shy, unworldly girl, with few wits about her. She would trip over the cordless phone, ask for a price check at the Pound Only store, and sit on the TV to watch the couch. She put stamps on her faxes, studied for blood tests, and once sold the car to get petrol money. Her mother was concerned that she would never marry and schooled her religiously in the fine art of attracting a man.

'Sweetheart! Men like dainty, well-mannered girls who keep a squeaky clean house,' her mother would say.

Rick was the male version of Mary Margaret. When asked to speak his mind he was speechless. He took a ruler to bed to see how long he slept, once tried to drown a fish and put 'Capricorn' on the line marked 'sign here' on a job application. He was looking to marry a girl just like the one Mary Margaret's mother described.

Rick met Mary Margaret at the newsagent's one day, remembered her from school and asked if he might call her. She invited him over for dinner the very next day. She was so demure, she cut her peas in half before she ate them, chewed each fifty times and dabbed at the corners of her mouth with her napkin. Rick was impressed until he saw her through the kitchen doorway slurping leftovers from the pot with the serving spoon. But, willing to give it another try, he stopped by one day with his colicky dog.

'Have you got a teaspoon of dust that I could give my dog to settle his stomach?' he asked Mrs Wilson.

'Oh, you'll not find any dust in this house,' the lady said proudly.

'Why, Mum,' said Mary Margaret, 'I bet you'll find a bucketful under my bed.'

End of romance.

The young girl hoped she might find true love with a stalwart individual rumoured to stand tall and proud with connections to Westminster. So she travelled to London with the hope of obtaining a meeting with the renowned figure admired by many, only to be crushed to learn that Big Ben was just a clock.

When she heard that 90% of all crime occurs around the home, she moved – to Florida – in search of sunshine. Disenchanted with the usual tourist haunts, she found peace in the quiet backwoods country near the Okeechobee swamp in the Everglades.

One day she walked into a store that specialised in alligator leather products. She gazed longingly at a pair of brown alligator pumps, then gasped aloud as she saw the $250 price tag.

'Wha, little lady. Those are the fahnest shoes in mah stoah. A real steal at that prahce,' said the shopkeeper.

'Well, stealing them is the only way I could afford those,' chirped Mary Margaret.

'Mebbe y'all could go out ta tha swamp and catch yo'sef a 'gator and make ya own shoes,' joked the shopkeeper. Mary Margaret smiled weakly and left.

Now the shopkeeper lived in the backwoods country himself. As he drove along the winding road home, he slammed on his brakes as he saw Mary Margaret waist-deep in the adjacent swampy waters. He rushed over and was thunderstruck as he saw the girl aim a double-barrelled shotgun at an alligator approaching her not ten feet away. With one blast the animal was dead and Mary Margaret dragged the animal and placed it on a pile of several others she had stacked on the swampbank.

'Lawdy me, little lady!' praised the astonished man as he gaped at the alligator pile, 'Now ya can have alla the 'gator shoes ya want.'

'You would think so, wouldn't you?' the confused girl replied. 'But, look. None of them are wearing any!!'

(Developed with the help of some very old jokes and a book called Storytellers: Stories and Legends from the South!*)*

April '99

Good Ol' Mare

As I waited for my friend, Mary, to emerge from the customs hall at Gatwick last week, a shiver of dread washed over me. I recalled the spring of 1989 when I was the traveller and she was my welcomer to the Atlanta, Georgia, airport. It was the first time in my life that I was returning to a place I had once lived, in the same healthy physical condition I had left in; I left slim in 1986 and was still slim. And I was being brought back, expenses paid, to share my slimming secrets with a group of people hoping to do the same. How I looked forward to the reunion! Now, ten years later, Mary would see me 50 pounds fatter than I was when she first met me, and I was already 50 pounds overweight at that time! My value to her as a human being and friend was sure to be diminished by my larger size.

Even though we had been in telephone contact in recent times and she was well aware of my eating woes and bodily expansion, I still cringed as I visualised her startled reaction at her first sight of me. (I deliberately positioned myself 20 yards from the doors so I wouldn't be the first person she'd see.) Each time someone other than Mary emerged, my heart would register an extra thump. It seemed to take forever. To soothe my anxiety I thought of Elizabeth Taylor, whose battles of the bulge have been made so public. Remember some years back when she regained a diminutive waist after many years of chubbiness? She was so excited and, wanting to share her good fortune with the world, she penned a book, *Elizabeth Takes Off*. As I

watched her get fat again, I could only imagine what it would feel like to widen in the public eye.

There she was! Mary, my short friend with the turned-up nose, heading my way looking just as much a pixie at 40 as she had at 30. A little pale and fatigued, she brightened as she saw me, no disgust on her face, no signs of sympathy or horror. As we embraced, ten years evaporated and here we were: good old Mare and good old Lin, together again. This was my safe harbour returned, one of the elite few who know that I eat dandruff and still love me. I forgot my ego as we found my car and the way to the M23.

It was my turn to delight in her wide-eyed wonder at the land around her, this newcomer to a land of kings and queens, the stomping ground of the Bard, the culinary home to provocative vittles like faggots and toad in the hole. I could see in her the wonder of a child in a new found fantasyland. I could see me four years ago. And, I thought, how lucky England is to have Mary in her bosom!

You see, Mary's really an angel in disguise. Mary is one of those rare people who brings out the best in everyone around her, but doesn't realise she is doing it. She knew exactly the right gifts to bring to my nine-year-old son, like the T-shirt that said 'Extreme Limit' with the funky androgynous alien on the skateboard. She was kind enough to say to me, 'You know, you probably don't notice' (and I didn't), 'but I'm 30 pounds heavier than I was when I saw you last,' as she offered me a Native American storybook called *Keepers of the Night*. She is single, without children of her own, yet she can be everyone's Mom, auntie or friend. Just two hours in my house, she checked my computer for any e-mail messages and, in less than 24 hours, her family and friends had already registered the severe withdrawal symptoms of a Mary-less existence!

She spent her first day with me packing up blankets for Kosovo refugees in a cold Bletchley school. She befriended the staff at the Wakefield Farm Shop, and enjoyed a fish 'n chip dinner at the home of my friend who was astounded to find in Mary another rock-collecting compadre and thrift shop junkie. The next day, we stopped in at the little Pury End shop and, within five minutes, she was invited out for a pub lunch. When I mentioned I couldn't go along, I was told, 'Oh, that's okay. We don't need you.'

She is in Brussels now visiting her homesick American cousin. 'I told her I would surprise her with some English spotted dick,' she chirped. 'Boy, is she guessing!' I miss Mary already!

May '99

Due to current political, economic and social constraints, the light at the end of the tunnel has been turned off until further notice

I saw this thought for the day posted in a nearby school staffroom the other day. It concisely reflects my thoughts as I read the morning paper on the Kosovo debacle and as I bundle bedding and basic toiletries for the refugees created by the disaster.

At least eight articulated lorries worth of donated goods need to be sorted through and repacked for shipment to Albania via Lightforce International, a charitable arm of the Milton Keynes Christian Centre with long-established ties to the region. As if it were not frustrating enough separating the usable donated items from the junk that some well-intentioned folks deem acceptable to give these refugees created by government folly, precious volunteer time has also been wasted cleaning up the rubble after five incidents of vandalism that have occurred at the school warehousing this food, clothing and other supplies.

I have not experienced so much anger with government since the Gulf War in 1990. Every time I go to the school as an atonement for NATO destruction, it feels like I'm putting a plaster on a hemorrhage. Which is why the special moments I have with the many children I tell stories to are all the more precious – flashes of light and hope at the end of the tunnel.

I have begun interpreting Shakespeare's plays in story form for middle and upper school pupils. The three-hour lesson plan includes a variety of interactive exercises to process the plays and awaken the adolescent pupil to the magic and rhythm of the language. Teachers have been delighted with the results thus far.

In one activity, after a discussion of the language patterns found in Shakespeare's plays, I ask pupils to take a facet of contemporary life and interpret it in 'Shakespeare-Speak'. I might suggest adapting Spice Girls' lyrics, writing a letter to a secret love, or giving a teacher a good excuse for failing to produce homework. The following is a description of a Big Mac hamburger developed by 11-year-old Charlotte (Lotty) Spurrell, a Year 6 pupil at Emerson Valley Combined School in Milton Keynes.

'Ye Big Mac' by Charlotte (Lotty) Spurrell

Thou mayest be pondering what, in truth, this repast known as 'Ye Big Mac' is. This task ist a great challenge, though I will accept and tell thee the best I can. There are many words in this humble world, yet few can describe this heavenly food of which you seek. 'Tis found in the house of McDonald's for a good price, not dear at all. In fact, neither arm nor leg must be forfeited to purchase this feast worthy of a king.

Now to the burger. Never hast thee tasted a food so divine. Its rich flavour flows through thee and warmest thee to the top of thy head down to thy feet. Prithee, let me explain to thee the mystery of the great burger. Imagine three pillows of soft, round bread, between nestle two rounds of succulent beef with sauce red as the blood shed upon the sword upon them. As if this were not sufficient, there is yet further delight to be had. Not one, but two pieces of moist, melting cheese. Finally, like jewels encrusted on a warrior's shield, the Big Mac is crowned

with sesame seeds scattered like dew on the early spring grass.
    And, now my friend, I've told you all.
    There's nothing more to say
    If thou desirest to taste this fayre
    Then hie thee there this day.

June '99

... *American Style*

I love trying products labelled *American Style*, because none of them resembles its counterpart I've used back home. The *American Style* muffin baking cases fit neither my American nor my British tins. The *American Candy* microwave popcorn packets produce a flavour unknown in any American cinema I've ever encountered. And the goop that Tesco suggests is *American Style* Ranch Salad Dressing is nothing like the creamy mayonnaise-buttermilk blend that graces USA dinner tables. So the only conclusion I can reach is that manufacturers of these products must be using *South* American or *Central* American recipes despite promoting their products with Stars & Stripes packaging.

I began thinking the other day that there are some *American Style* affectations I'd welcome in a minute. Such as . . .

American Style Queuing Etiquette. Picture this. A long queue of seven shoppers moves toward till #1 at a British Superstore. The head cashier decides to open till #2 to relieve the crowding. She sends a cashier to till #2. In the process, the last shopper in queue #1 immediately cuts over to the newly opened till, effectively taking the place the first shopper in queue #1 rightly deserves. In most USA stores the new cashier for till #2 would automatically guide the first in line at till #1 to her new position. Others behind her or him could then choose which till to wait for.

American Style Car Parks where you have enough room to open your door as you exit without hitting the car next to you.

American Style Letter Box Slots in countryside postboxes which will accept an A4 size envelope without the sender having to crumple it up.

American Style Cling Film/Foil Boxes with serrated edges sharp enough to indeed tear the product off the roll without demolishing the box. Add to this sandwich and food storage boxes that actually release one bag at a time instead of all 50.

American Style Highway Patrol Cars (I never thought I'd say this) that carry police officers who actually ticket a driver carrying out a dangerous manoeuvre, instead of weakly flashing their high beam lights – 'Naughty, naughty!'

American Style Directness. The most irritating British colloquialism I've come across is the ubiquitous 'I don't mind'.

'Would you like coffee or tea?'
'I don't mind.'
'It's no trouble to make either.'
'I don't mind.'
'Look, the kettle is on. Which do you want?'
'You're sure it's no bother?'
'No.'
'All right. Coffee then, if you're sure you don't mind.'
'Aaaaaaaaaagggghhh!'

Now, to be fair, there are some American aspects of life I wouldn't wish on the British or anyone else for that manner, such as . . .

American Style Treatment of Young Adults. If you leave school at 16 years of age you are considered a ne'er-do-well dropout, destined never to leave the fast food counter of employment. No equivalent of respectable GCSE certificates go with you. Yet, like most other 16-year-olds, you can still obtain a driving licence. So you can operate a four-wheeled lethal weapon, and perhaps be permitted to purchase a semi-automatic gun. But you also will know it is a criminal activity to consume alcoholic beverages in most states until you are 21. Many young people find themselves in a police state on a Saturday night as they are often

pursued by law enforcers sanctioned by the community to crack down on teenaged drinking and driving while their parents might be on their third martini at a house party around the corner. However, if you want to vote, marry or serve in the Armed Forces, copulate and propagate, you are considered responsible enough at age 18. Go figure it!

American Style Table Manners. I loved watching you all eat when I first moved here. Your knife has complete partnership with your fork in consuming a meal. I had often heard about the European style of eating, but until I actually saw you shovelling those peas onto your forks with your dancing knives, until I saw your left hands spear your meat with those same forks as your right hands still gripped your knives, I could only imagine the experience. You see, we Americans have a very peculiar notion of proper eating. Say you've got in front of you a lovely piece of roasted meat.

A. One uses one's knife merely to cut no more than four bits of meat at a time. We rest the knife on the edge of the plate while we transfer the fork out of the holding-the-meat-steady-piercing position in one hand to the eating position in other hand. Which hand one uses is based on whether you are left or right-handed.

B. We eat our no-more-than-four bites of meat, transfer the fork back to the other hand into holding-the-meat-steady-piercing position, pick up the knife with our cutting hand and repeat 'A'.

C. At no time is a knife or a hunk of bread acceptably used to ease our veggies onto our forks. One must only spear with the fork or lamely slide it around hoping to catch the last morsel of mashed potatoes or sweet corn. For shame if you use your free thumb!

D. When one is eating solo or in the bosom of one's own family, one may ignore the above!

July/August '99

How I Spent My Summer Vacation

I left a month early for the States this year on 'personal business', I informed most acquaintances. My few close friends knew the exact details. They knew how much my destructive eating behaviour was affecting every part of my life; they knew I had progressed into an eating pattern way beyond the scope of conventional diet approaches; they knew I was a food addict; they knew I was entering a residential treatment program. I had been in a similar program back in 1984–85 on an outpatient basis with dramatic results lasting several years and, when research into what was available in England led to a dead end, I pursued options back in the USA.

A phone call last winter to a former therapist/nutritional counsellor offered me several leads – most of them exorbitantly expensive and heavy on the head-shrinking. But one of my calls resulted in contact with a place called Crutcher's Serenity House, named after founder Bob Crutcher and located only a short distance from my home in northern California. Its usual clients are alcoholics and drug addicts, with a sprinkling of compulsive gamblers. When I outlined my eating history to the clinical director there, he listened patiently and suggested that Crutcher's could offer me the help I needed. The cooks would follow whatever eating regimen my nutritionist designed for me in the protective custody of the house, while I would be treated in all other respects just like the other addicts. As he continued to describe the program philosophy, I saw that it bore a striking resemblance to what I had experienced before, and

I felt at home. But I had a major concern. In places like Crutcher's, I knew that group identification and interaction was at the heart of the recovery model. 'But what about the other clients?' I asked. 'Could they accept me as one of them? They might not put the abuse of ice cream or Chinese food on the same scale as gin and cocaine.'

'Well, since you would be our first eating disorder without an alcohol or drug problem attached, it's hard to say what the initial reaction might be,' I was told. 'But I am confident that our approach here can minimise those kinds of hiccups. We see your problem as acting out the same addictive behaviour as the rest of our residents.'

With the cost being just a fraction of what the other programs charged, and encouraged by my family's support, I put myself into the care of my nutritionist and Serenity House with complete abandon for the standard 28 days on June 23rd. Beaten down by my food compulsion and the months of preparation for the journey, and wary of hoping too hard that even this drastic action could help me, I cautiously greeted the ten other residents sitting on the patio of this large but modest house ironically situated in the heart of California wine country. As the staff searched my bags for contraband alcohol and drugs, then proceeded to confiscate my mouthwash and perfume, I collapsed on my new bed, burst into tears and wanted to run. Little did I know that, in the days and weeks to come, my life would be enriched beyond measure as I was separated from compulsive eating one more time.

As my body was fed life-supporting meals, I learned that certain foods are for me just as toxic as alcohol is to an alcoholic. I learned from daily experience, as food cravings disappeared, skin problems vanished, depression lifted and robust physical energy was restored, that *what* I had been eating was causing me just as many problems as the emotional, psychological roots of the compulsion. I was bombarded with lectures about the addictive personality and group sessions with my peers that exposed my faulty ways of thinking, including obsessive preoccupation with

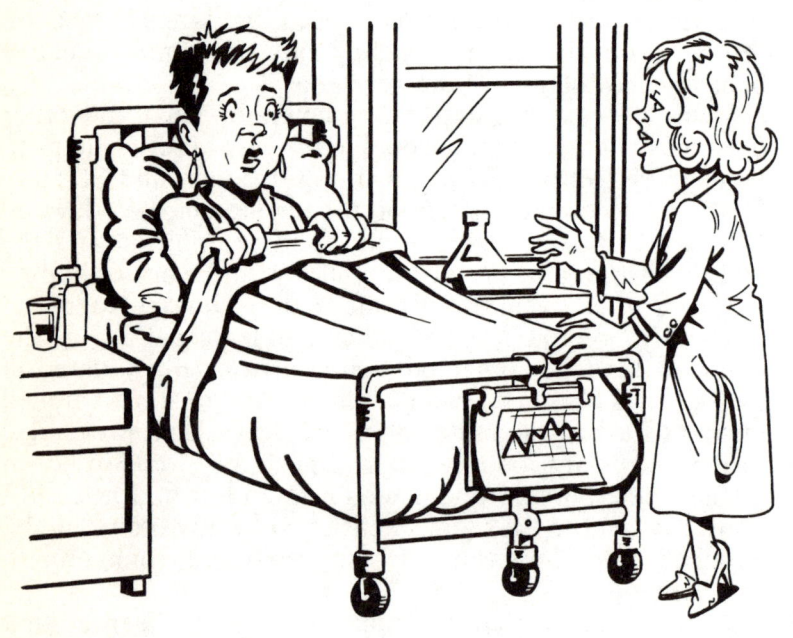

weight and body image. Any doubts that I was different from the other addicts around me were quickly dispelled. And as they came to know me and my bizarre eating saga, they came to believe I belonged. I learned how difficult it is for a bunch of compulsive people to live and work together. I saw the pain of young heroin addicts in their early days of detox. I felt the limits on my freedoms as my days were programmed for me and movements restricted. And I began to feel a true delight in living once more, the same delight I experience whenever I tell a story.

It was probably no coincidence that the two cooks and I became good friends. They took great care with my food preparation and presentation. And since there weren't many other women residents at the time, we shared more deeply as well. I learned that one of them was a cancer survivor, and I marvelled at her good humour and kind demeanor. She is becoming a role model for me in more ways than one.

In the difficult days of re-entry into the real world after my release from Crutcher's, I had a mammogram to evaluate a small lump I had discovered in my right breast a few months before. The British mammogram I had in March in response to this discovery showed no abnormalities, but I still felt uneasy. The more recent test definitely showed a suspicious growth and, last week, I had a lumpectomy which confirmed that it was cancerous.

So my summer holiday in the States is continuing with further testing to establish that no cancer is present in other body parts, and more surgery is scheduled next week to verify that no cancer is present in the lymph nodes. As far as cancer goes, I've got a fairly common variety and prognosis is excellent for a full recovery. I hope to complete the diagnostics here, have the cancer treatment protocol outlined by my American doctors, and then have the treatment implemented by their British counterparts when I return to England in mid-September.

I am homesick for the English countryside, my dog and friends. But I am overwhelmed with gratitude for a clear head defogged at the moment from compulsive eating, for being allowed to experience this new bend in the road in the company of dear friends and family, for all the available support in the community here for cancer patients. I am especially grateful to a nurse who has passed on to me a funny little book written by a breast cancer survivor and entitled *Not Now – I'm Having a No Hair Day*. Whatever the future may bring in treating my own breast cancer, I hope I can face it with just this kind of humour.

September '99

Overexposed

On more than one occasion since my last piece I have asked myself why I did it. Why did I feel compelled to tell three villages about my food and cancer traumas? Why didn't I just write about the subtle differences in women's public toilets east and west of the Atlantic like I originally planned?

On one level, I think I wanted to avoid dealing with the inevitable comments when one loses weight, like 'Oh, you've lost quite a bit of weight. How are you doing it?'. In my former slimming periods, I used to enjoy responding to comments like that with a detailed description of everything I was eating at the time, as if it was a new-found panacea for the world's ills. But I've returned to compulsive eating too many times in my life to be that flippant anymore. As I savour each passing day free of the food obsession, I feel a much quieter form of gratitude for the emotional and physical overhaul that intensive treatment provided me this summer. Sharing that with you I think underscored the stakes for me – eating well and caring for my dysfunctional machine of a body is not just an option but a necessity for my future health and sanity. And, if in social situations, I stick to my herbal teas, you would know why it's just that important for me to do so.

In that same vein, I wanted you to know about my cancer, so if you saw me on the street with a bald head, you would know why and not be afraid to speak with me. Already I have met some familiar faces in the village and I can see that people are hesitant to say the word 'cancer' as if it

might depress me. Instead they have said, 'I was sorry to hear about your problem', or 'I read about your situation in the *Old Mail*'. It really is all right for you to say the word 'cancer', because that's what I've got, and facing it in a direct manner is most therapeutic for me. And when *I* say it, it breaks through my own fear and denial. How can I face the difficult months ahead if I ignore reality?

And part of my hope in sharing all this with you is that there is something special and intimate that happens between people when vulnerable, secret selves are brought into the open. We all have these corners of ourselves that harbour shame, guilt, fear and sadness. Corners we like to hide in which sometimes keep us lonely and isolated as we fear that no others could possibly be experiencing the same feelings. When one person comes out of hiding, it often helps others to leave their corners as well and perhaps find some humour along the way.

Here's a Chinese parable that I look to many times when the going gets rough and I think I know what's best for me. And I especially dedicate it to my new friend, Helen:

There once was a man who owned a horse and cart. He earned his living hauling goods to and from the distant market for all the people in his village. One day his horse ran away and all the villagers came to him to lament his loss.

The man told them, 'Well, it may be bad, it may be good. I do not know.'

The next day the horse returns with another horse from the wild following behind it. Now all the villagers marvelled at his tremendous good fortune at now having two horses instead of one.

'Well, it may be good, it may be bad. I do not know,' the man replied.

The next day the man's son is thrown from the wild horse as he attempts to train it. His leg is badly broken from the fall. The villagers soothe the man since his son is a support to the business.

From the man, calmly: 'May be bad, may be good. I do not know.'

The next day the local war lord storms the village and conscripts all the able-bodied young men. The man's son is spared because of his broken leg. The villagers remind the man how lucky he is that this son was spared.

You know the man's reply. I say the same about my cancer and my eating disorder. And enough about that already. I'll discuss the women's toilets next time.

October '99

Loo Habits

Most females at some point in their lives have wet their bottoms in toilet (that's *toilet*, not *toilette*) water due to the failure of the males in their lives to put the seat back down after use. Those of us with young sons have had the dubious pleasure of the experience after they have forgotten to flush besides. Some of us have had the added bonus of sitting on a wet seat because sleepy little boys have forgotten to put the seat *up*. And most women know that all males from time to time need to mark their territory by spraying on the walls. It's always easy to know when one walks into a strange household if the majority of residents are male; use the loo and smell the disinfectant.

Personally, I think that women should be in control of their own toilet habits. It's just as easy for us to put the seat down as it is for the guys to lift it up. The rest of the above are minor little annoyances we bear for the pleasure of having men in our lives.

During my extended stay in the USA this past summer, I noticed some subtle differences in women's public toilets there as opposed to those in the UK. Most of the feminine hygiene products machines actually work in the UK. And their disposal is caught by much nicer bins – you don't actually have to see everybody else's as you toss yours in. My only gripe concerns teachers' loos in UK schools. They usually put a bin in one stall only, not in the stall I usually pick.

US stalls are much wider, the seats much sturdier and the openings in the bottom of the stalls easier to pass toilet roll through should you need to ask your neighbour to share her bounty. But new US stall construction sadly reflects the deteriorating state of loo etiquette; the hooks fastened to the inside of the doors to accommodate carry bags, handbags and coats are now belly-high rather than at eye-level. New-age thieves have mastered the art of reaching over the top of a loo door to nick a purse on a high-placed hook before the poor victim has even had a chance for a quick wipe!

We also have these paper seat cover dispensers, though only high-class loos actually *have* the seat covers in them. The idea is to provide you with the confidence to actually sit down on the seat, your sensitive bottom protected from nasty germs. One then just flushes away the seat cover with the other waste. I surmise that it's the same women who gripe about men leaving the seat up who also don't flush down their seat covers, leaving them for the next users to deal with gingerly.

And Americans like choice. Some toilets have electric hand drying machines *and* paper towels. Many have just paper towels, which is why their floors are usually littered with them when employee 'Cindy' has not been in at her appointed time to tidy up. And given the availability of paper towels, you'd think that American women would wipe down their sink areas when they were finished using them. But, you're just as likely to get your handbag wet on an American public toilet sink as in one in the UK. Then again, you can brush your teeth, cup your hands with water for a mouth rinse and not have to stick your face in the electric dryer.

There seem to be some behaviours common to women on both sides of the Atlantic. Women who pee standing up with the seat down and who refuse to wipe their seats afterwards are even more annoying than the little boys who forget to put the seats up. At least the boys can use being three years old as an excuse. Maybe those women are marking their territory like men do. And isn't it bizarre that women would rather wait in a long queue than to use a stall whose door is missing? Men willingly wave their willies in front of each other as they stand side by side. But, after all, for them it's just a matter of unzipping a zip, doing one's business and giving a little shake, isn't it?

November '99

* Note: The Old Mail editors declined to publish this piece, deeming it too offensive for village sensibilities. This from a citizenry regularly exposed to the most abhorrent selection of toilet humour I've ever seen in the greeting card section of any local newsagent or card shop.

Internet Humour

The advent of e-mail in my life has rejuvenated many dormant relationships, from relatives to old college buddies. All of us seem to share a delight in passing on humourous anecdotes when we come upon them. As my own creativity seems to be taking a nap since my November column (on the differences between American and UK public toilets) was rejected by *Old Mail* editors as too distasteful for public consumption, I'll share with you instead a bit of Americana e-mailed to me by my favourite aunt in Florida. These are 'bloopers' taken from various church newsletters.

The Scouts are saving aluminium cans and bottles to be recycled. Proceeds will be used to cripple children.

The outreach committee has enlisted 25 visitors to make calls on people who are not afflicted with any church.

Ladies Bible Study will be held Thurs. morning at 10. Lunch will follow after the B.S. is done.

Low Self-esteem Support Group meets Thurs. at 7 pm. Please use the back door.

The pastor will preach his farewell message, after which the choir will sing 'Break Forth into Joy'.

Remember in prayer the many who are sick of our church and community.

Due to the Rector's illness, Monday's healing service will be discontinued until further notice.

Don't let worry kill you. Let the Church help.

Come to the Sunday evening potluck supper. Prayer and medication will follow.

An ice cream social will be held Tuesday at 4 pm. All ladies giving milk please come early.

This afternoon there will be a meeting in the south and north ends of the church. Children will be baptised at both ends.

This being Easter Sunday, we will ask Mrs. Lewis to come forward and lay an egg at the altar.

A special collection will be taken to defray the cost of the new carpet. All those wishing to do something on the new carpet will come forward and get a piece of paper.

The Senior Choir invites any member of the congregation who enjoys sinning to join the choir.

At the evening service tonight, the sermon topic will be 'What is hell?' Come early and listen to our choir practice.

The 1999 Spring Retreat will be hell May 20 & 21.

A bean supper will be held Sunday evening in the church hall. Music to follow . . .

For those of you who have children and don't know it, we have a nursery downstairs.

Mrs Crutchfield and Mrs Rankin sang a duet at the church meeting the other day. The Lord Knows Why.

From a little boy reciting the Lord's Prayer. 'Lead us not into the station and deliver us some e-mail.'

Amen, and Merry Christmas!

December '99–January '00

At War with My Major and Minor Appliances

When we first arrived in England four and a half years ago, we entered the realm of 240 volts. Though we brought along a few big-ticket items like a TV, VCR and stereo equipment with their corresponding transformers, we had to purchase the rest of our electrics quickly without much chance of comparison shopping. It was probably due to my pleasant experience buying them at Currys that I stupidly had the expectation that these items would continue working past the 1-year warranty expiry date, so I dismissed the sales pitch for extended warranties as a ploy to separate me from additional money without good reason. I thought of my 15-year-old washer-tumble dryer set and my 10-year-old fridge still humming along in my California garage and, figuring we had such a finite stay here, why worry?

    I should have suspected trouble when I noticed that the magnetic seals on my new fridge and freezer did not adhere properly in places. Not a major difficulty, but still energy-inefficient. The repairman brought along two new doors to solve the problem, but when he looked at the units, he smiled and said, 'Have you got any kitchen roll, luv?' Feeling very bright for already knowing that kitchen roll meant paper towels and that he wasn't asking for bread, I watched as he cleverly filled in the gaps by stuffing bits of paper towels inside the rubber housing covering the seals. Problem solved! 'I'll go ahead and leave you the new doors just in case you might need them.' They are still in the cellar, but during the time since, the flimsy plastic veggie preserver in the fridge has cracked, and I regularly have problems with some items freezing when I accidentally cover up that hole in the back of the interior underscored by the dire warning 'Keep drain clear'. And I lament the loss of the tempered glass shelves in my USA fridge when something here spills on the top shelf and the dripping liquid covers everything below it through the gaps in the metal shelves.

But at least these items still work fairly well. The toaster still works when I hold down the lever manually. The tumble dryer still works, though it takes two hours to run through the cycle and only when it's filled to half-capacity. The microwave still works, though I can see the clock/timer only when the kitchen is dark. I am on my second washing machine, tea kettle, coffee-maker, hand-mixer and vacuum. When the first vacuum died I decided to buy the bagless wonder with 'dual cyclone' action. It needed two replacement parts in the first six months, and I regularly have to take it apart to clear out the clumps of dirt that inhibit the suction.

Some of you may think I have discarded perfectly good appliances because I didn't check the fuse in the plug. Sorry to disappoint you. I learned about fused plugs early on.

My saga with blenders is the best. First it was a British brand that died. Then I got a French one – French name, the French are renowned for their cooking, what could be more logical? Wrong! Cheap plastic housing for the blade assembly cracked early on – still usable but leaks. This past autumn, I noticed another British model on sale at Tesco. Good price, stainless steel housing, large-capacity glass container instead of plastic. Now people had told me this company's products are the best, the pride of Britain. So I eagerly brought it home, creamed the leek soup and was optimistic that this would be my last blender! A few weeks of happy use lulled me into a false sense of security when the inevitable occurred just as I was ready to puree. The switch wouldn't turn. I had a banger of a car about 20 years

ago that often responded to gentle verbal persuasion when it wouldn't start. 'Bessie' we called her. Well, this blender was no Bessie. My gentle persuasion turned to heated expletives and, as I found myself fuming while forcing the misbehaving switch to move when it stubbornly refused, I screamed the scream of a consumer wronged, causing my young son to dash to the kitchen in fear of some awful cancer consequence. 'No, Sweetie, just Mom fighting with the blender.' So back to the manufacturer it went and out came the leaky French one which lumbers along this very day.

There is room for optimism. It finally dawned on me that the best appliance I've used is one that came with my rental house – the German-made dishwasher. Once I figured out the benefits of citric acid and dishwasher salt in enhancing its smooth operation, it has never failed me. So when it came time to buy that new washing machine, the replacement coffee-maker and hand-mixer, I bypassed the competition and bought German. So far, so good!

February '00

'You'll Go Bald, You Know!'

Such were the delicately phrased words spoken by my American oncologist as we discussed the effects of my future chemotherapy last summer. Right then and there, I decided that, once the first tuft of hair fell onto my pillow, drifted onto my shoulder, rubbed off on my towel or settled into my mouth – off the rest would go! If I was going to be bald eventually, I wanted to be the one in charge of the process. It gave me the creeps to think about the systematic deterioration of my hair follicles, victims of an insidious assault by the medicines designed to help me. I wanted to see those drugs as rivers of healing. Losing my hair at a rate and in a pattern I couldn't predict would only create an image of myself falling apart. I never saw my hair as any big asset anyway – thin, mousy brown and greying fast. Bald could be an improvement, especially since I knew I wasn't the wig type.

Of course, it was easy to be so bold before the fact, but almost three weeks after my first chemo treatment, I casually ran my hand through my hair and there were the strands on my fingers. My parents were here to support me through the beginning days and, as I showed my mother the evidence, I declared that I was calling a hairdresser that very day for a shave. Visibly upset, Mother cautioned me to wait – to wait until after she returned home so she wouldn't have to see her daughter's head naked. Just then, the phone rang, a friend calling to see how I was doing. When I told her of my intentions, she volunteered to go along with me to the hairdresser. It gave me an idea for a head-shaving ceremony. I called another friend who was free that day and she agreed to join us. As I began to get excited, my mother perked up and asked if she could come as well. So armed with a few bottles of an herbal, champagne-like drink, paper cups and a camera, off we went.

The salon staff knew why I was requesting the shave and were upbeat and anxious to please. So, with my loved ones around me and the camera ready, out came the clippers. In no time at all, my wispy locks drifted away and I sat facing the bare, stubbly facts. 'It suits you, you look ten years younger' was the universal reply. I wasn't so sure, but we raised our bubbly-filled paper cups to toast the liberation of my head and good health to all. I kept the last strand the clippers touched.

Still, the stubble bothered me; I wanted the smooth, shiny look. But I was afraid to use a razor on my scalp. A friend gave me a hair-removal cream for sensitive skin. I showed it to my doctor who gave his okay, but what do doctors know anyway? It didn't work very well and left me with a series of blisters that began where my hairline met the forehead and continued around to the nape of the neck. A few well-placed screws and I could have been Frankenstein's bride. So I chose a woman's safety razor with a mild shaving cream next time and I've been using this method ever since to shave twice a week. Yes, I was surprised, too, that stubble appears quickly, even on a head compromised by chemotherapy. I often wonder what my head would have looked like if I had allowed the hair to fall out on its own.

Although I was shown creative ways to use scarves and sashes to shroud the baldness in public, I decided that bald is what I am right now, so bald I would be. So I just cover my head when it gets cold with a selection of hats that blend with the clothing I happen to be wearing. I have two favourite polartec ski caps that I wear in my house when the drafts give me a chill. But indoors in public places and while I'm working, I just go bald. I suppose a little black leather along with some nose, lip and eyebrow piercing

could give me a certain fashionable look, but most people just give me a little extra stare and go about their business. The children I tell stories to are direct in asking me why I have no hair. I tell them that some medicine I'm taking has caused my hair to fall out and that I shave my head regularly to keep it smooth and shiny. That's enough for them.

In writing about chemotherapy-induced baldness, I must confess that the hair loss is not restricted to the head. Can you get the picture when I speak of the loss of *all* body hair? Since I've already had seven of my scheduled eight chemo sessions, the deforestation is fairly complete. And do you know which hair loss is the most annoying? Not the one you might think of first! It's the lack of nose hair. I never before appreciated the function of my nose hair in keeping the mucous bits down to manageable size. My bogeys now know no sense of proportion!

MY TOP TEN REASONS WHY BEING HAIRLESS AIN'T SO BAD

1. The dosh I save on shampoo, conditioner and hair gel, I use on sweet-smelling massage oil for my head. I only have to use the blow dryer on the wet dog.
2. I am one of the lucky few women who know exactly where the dents are on my head.
3. My big earrings look even bigger.
4. People rub my head for good luck.
5. I can hide in the melon case in the superstore and give some unsuspecting soul a real surprise!
6. The temptation for extramarital flirting is minimised since there are no eyelashes to flutter.
7. I don't have to pluck out those little grey chin hairs that had the nerve to appear on my pre-menopausal face.
8. When the time comes for the bald giant to reveal himself in one of my stories, I can really play the part.
9. I can go for a drive on a balmy day with the windows

down and the breeze on my face without messing up my hair.
10. I can remove a plaster without the added sting of body hair coming along with it.

March '00

The Yank is Going Back

It was inevitable. I knew my husband's job would end eventually and we would return to the States. We are. In June. Only the USA doesn't feel like home anymore. I just returned from a mission there to ready my house for our impending arrival. Good friends who had been our tenants have already moved and it seemed prudent to have some needed repairs done while the house is vacant.

As I made my way out of the San Francisco airport, the big news story on the radio concerned Americans' indignation that the price of gasoline had risen to more than $1.50 a gallon. That's less than a pound. President Clinton was considering using domestic oil reserves to meet the 'crisis'. Since the British price of petrol is about £3.50 ($5.60) a gallon, it was hard for me to have any sympathy, especially since most of the cars around me on the freeway would be hard-pressed to get 20 miles to the gallon. I saw all the hubbub as another example of how ignorant Americans are of the world around them. Do we somehow have divine rights to cheap petrol? I was ignorant, too, before my European adventure began. I remember a phone conversation I had with my husband when he preceded us to England in May of '95. I actually asked him, 'Do they have hot water over there?'

I am in turmoil. I love it here. My life has been enriched beyond measure here. My ten-year-old son has done well in his little school. But my older sons are now all in the States. They have had no home to retreat to on long weekends, and seeing them only once or twice a year is not enough for

me. I'll miss the simple things like watching the same bottle of bubble bath make its way from tombola to tombola, yet I'll be glad to once again get my laundry washed and dried in an hour. My new friends here hold such a big piece of my heart, how can I stand not seeing their faces regularly? Yet I thought the same thing when I said goodbye to my buddies in California nearly five years ago. I'll miss the ease of reserving cinema seats by phone, yet I'll be happy to once again pick fresh oranges from my backyard trees. I'll long for the vistas of the English countryside when the rape is in full colour, but I'll be happy to see the sunshine on a regular basis.

I can't leave just yet! I haven't seen Cornwall, Bath or the moors. I haven't been to Italy. I haven't gotten thin yet. I haven't learned to like Christmas pudding or instant coffee. I haven't seen a coronation or been to Parliament for a lesson in rude behaviour.

But I have had coronation chicken and learned that you *eat* a cream tea as well as drink it. I've seen the death of a princess and the dawning of a new century. I've had a pheasant pay me a visit through the dog flap, lay an egg in my kitchen and then pass out on the settee. I now know that a pantomime is not an evening of Marcel Marceau. I've been able to watch the BBC period dramas before my American friends get to see them. I know that you never call a bum bag a fanny pack here, but you can run over sleeping policemen. I've actually been in a conservatory and now know that they are not just places to hide the rope or the knife while playing Cluedo. I've been to Shakespeare's home and heard Beethoven's 9th Symphony at the Albert Hall. I've listened to a tirade against Americans from a French cabdriver in Lyons as he collected me from The Museum of the Resistance, a sobering place underscoring the complicity of the Vichy government in Nazi persecution. (The irony of his self-righteousness as we left this monument to an embarrassing piece of French history was somehow lost to the driver.) I've undergone cancer treatment here. I've brought a little bit of joy to several thousand children in a basketful of stories.

In the coming weeks, I'll have time to pause and reflect on the joys and sorrows of the last few years as I go through the house weeding out the junk from what I want to keep. Which children's drawings of my stories should I throw away as they have faded on my study wall? Which bric-a-brac picked up at jumble sales should I discard? What should I sell or give away? I know from my many moves how time causes memories to fade, how contacts with friends left behind diminish over the years. How the loss of identity with one community is just as powerful as the excitement of establishing one in a new community. Will leaving behind the can of tuna given to me by some special children in response to a story make me forget faster? I don't want to forget the life I've had here.

The Dalai Lama has said, 'Remember that not getting what you want can be a great stroke of luck.' I don't want this move right now, but then I didn't want to move to England either when my husband first asked. Somebody remind me how lucky I am!

April '00
(This series will officially end with the July/August issue, five full years after it began)

To Be a Hero

When I was about 12 years old, a plane disabled by icing on its wings crashed into the Potomac River bordering Washington DC. It was a severely cold winter's day there with grey skies and freezing rain. I can't remember the number of casualties or whether the pilot deliberately negotiated a landing there to avoid more tragic loss of life on city streets.

That afternoon, my view of life irrevocably changed as a favourite TV soap opera was pre-empted by live crash coverage. The TV cameras focused on survivors floundering in the river as a helicopter hovered overhead lowering a rescue chair. The rescue team already in the water was hampered by the high winds and icy, choppy waters. A number of spectators watched from a nearby bridge. The cameras focused on one woman, who later turned out to be a flight attendant, as she struggled to grab the helicopter lifeline. Each time she reached for it, the winds would sweep it from her grasp. A man from the crowd on the bridge suddenly leaped into the water, swam to the woman and helped her on to the chair. He remained in the water, providing assistance to other victims as well.

That man was not a firefighter or policeman, not a daredevil who ordinarily lived on the edge. He was just your everyday Joe trying to live a good life like the rest of us. Out of the crowd of people watching from the bridge, why was he the only one who took action? What was it about him that allowed him to forget his own safety and leap into the frigid water?

In the aftermath of the accident, as he was honoured with

medals and accolades, he answered those questions in the typical way most heroes do: 'Well, I just saw what needed to be done and I did it.'

Since that time, I have been in awe of those who rush into burning buildings to save a stranger, who walk out on a building's edge to prevent a suicide, who crawl into an unstable mine shaft to rescue a trapped colleague. Because, out of all the twisted messages I got from my religious education as the frailties of human nature often perverted the teachings of Jesus, the one that no one could taint was 'Greater love hath no man than this, that a man lay down his life for his friends.' (John ch. 15 v. 13)

As a young girl and as an adult, I have always wondered what I would do if faced with this kind of challenge. I've secretly fantasised about it, seen myself pushing a child out of the way of an oncoming car. In the ultimate hero scenario, I either die or walk away without anyone knowing what I have done. It's not the dream of receiving public recognition for such a bold deed that motivates this fantasy, but the notion that I would finally be right with God. That such an act would give me absolution for all the times I ignored the homeless person in the doorway, drove by the woman with three kids as she tried to deal with her flat tyre or turned the page of the newspaper that pictured a starving African child. I could atone for the times I plunked my child in front of the telly in order to do some really important task like the laundry, the times I made excuses for hanging up the phone because a friend's distress was too overwhelming, the times I diminished another's soul by idle gossip, the times I lied to cover my mistakes.

Yesterday, as I made my way home on the A43 from radiation therapy in Oxford, I found myself trailing a car carrier loaded with new Fords of various sizes and models. In the course of a few miles, it had rained and hailed. As we entered a passing zone, the car carrier and I proceeded to pass a smaller lorry. I was startled by and somewhat annoyed at the speed the huge vehicle in front of me managed to achieve and, for a split second, imagined what would happen should the driver lose control. As a road sign indicated we were merging back into a single lane, I sped up to pass the car carrier, but could not safely do it, so I reluctantly stayed behind, whingeing that my forward vision was still limited.

As we entered Silverstone and reduced our speed, the car carrier rear-ended a large Land Rover, throwing it right into oncoming traffic before it settled into the pub drive where it had been headed before impact. The car carrier swerved and swayed dangerously, jumping the left kerb and landing safely on the grass and parallel to the road, its front wheels nearly buried in the mud as it came to a stop. Though it leaned left, it seemed stable. No other vehicles were involved.

The two young men who occupied the smashed Land Rover sprang from their car, apparently uninjured, as I pulled my car over the kerb in front of the car carrier. As I walked toward its massive hulk, I wondered how the driver fared behind its shattered windscreen. Would I find a face covered with blood, would I be able to help? As I reached his door, I noticed some fluid leaking from the undercarriage beneath him, but luckily it was just windscreen wash. The driver was shaken but unharmed, muttering over and over how he had not seen the Land Rover waiting to turn right, and how the whole thing was his fault. He was visibly relieved that the other passengers were not hurt. People from the pub emerged to offer assistance, with one employee joining me next to the transporter. Once we established that the driver was okay, the pub employee turned his attention to removing glass and metal from the road. Traffic could continue on.

While there was no need for my heroics this day, I could see that the distraught driver needed some help to make his next move. He could not exit from his side of the cab, so I encouraged him to come out the other side. He had to be careful to avoid bits of windscreen that covered the cab's interior. When he emerged, I helped to brush off the glass that covered his head and shirt, and just stood there offering kind words as he changed his shirt and shoes. As we stood there in the misty rain, we marvelled that no one seemed hurt and that no other vehicles were involved in the accident on the busy road filled with travellers making their way to the Easter Grand Prix. Equally amazing, all of the shiny new Fords continued to shine before us.

After leaving my name and address with the police, I discovered that the two young men in the Rover were in Silverstone to work at the race, had contacts there and would be taken care of. One of them, whose father had loaned them his Rover for the big weekend, made a superior effort to hold his temper as the car carrier driver apologised profusely.

Mobile phones were whisked out and necessary calls made. It was the first accident the transporter driver had ever been in. I offered him my name and phone number in case he needed a place to stay for the night, though I figured his employer would be making arrangements for his retrieval from the scene.

I gave him a hug, returned to my car and reflected on all the what ifs. If I had succeeded in passing him earlier, would I have found myself stopped behind the Land Rover when the transporter driver made his mistake? Would he have avoided the same mistake? Suppose it was fuel instead of windscreen wash flowing from the cab's undercarriage? What if an oncoming car had hit the Land Rover as it was pushed into traffic by the impact? What if I had found a badly injured driver behind the smashed windscreen?

No, this wasn't my day to be a hero, nor was it anyone else's in the vicinity. But maybe those of us in this tiny frame of time and circumstance learned something about humility, I about delivering a little tender loving care, the car carrier driver as he faced his responsibility in causing the crash, the Land Rover driver as he kept his temper in check.

And as for being right with God, well, that's probably a never-ending story.

May '00

The Final Hours

This is it. My life as an American expatriate on British soil is coming to an end. I've reviewed the Yank columns that have gone before and I want to bring them all together in a dynamic piece that will dazzle you with unforgettable insights into the human condition. I want you to remember me as one of the good guys whose humble words have resulted in profound changes in your view of America and the world.

No wonder I'm still sitting here after eight hours with the computer equivalent of a wastebasket full of crumpled paper.

I'll just tell you about two experiences I haven't mentioned before.

I was in England only two weeks when I went to my first flower show at a nearby church. I had never been in a 400-year-old building before, and never one brimming with flowers from genuine English country gardens. I snapped dozens of pictures and drifted over to the tea tent behind the church. I figured the best way to introduce myself was to praise the beauty of the flower arrangements and offer to help serve the tea. My offer was politely declined, but I was asked by the friendly lady in charge to 'Come round for coffee sometime, and I'll show you my garden.' Whoopee! My first friend. She gave me her phone number, probably not really expecting me to call. I did and invited myself over within a week. After a brief tour of her magnificent garden and greenhouse, we settled in the conservatory for our coffee. Aware of British reticence from reading about it in my 'Welcome to Great Britain' tour guide, I was determined to let her take the lead in our conversation and not push her into intimacy right away. And lead she did. I nearly spit out my coffee as she began telling me the story of her life, including details of her unusual sexual activities, where, when and with whom. So this was the great British reserve I had heard so much about. As we parted, I gave her my phone number so that we could meet again, but perhaps she regretted her candour, as we have never crossed paths since.

A few months into my stay I tried to learn to ride – a horse that is. But I didn't try too hard. I think my efforts were sabotaged by my basic belief that horses are meant to roam free and not be left in little cubicles until humans are ready to jump on their backs and manipulate them. Sounds noble, huh? Truth be known, I'm deathly afraid of them, their big teeth and the change of altitude one experiences while sitting on their backs. But I kept passing the beasts on the road and they seemed nice enough, so I decided to enrol in a small class at a nearby stables. My instructor took one look at me in my baggy sweater and leggings and immediately knew I needed a mounting block. I was so proud of myself once I sat in the saddle, but where was the saddle horn to hold on to? I'm sure the Lone Ranger had a saddle horn. But he wasn't English, was he? There was no alternative but to hold onto the reins. After a few minutes, I boldly reached over and gave my horse a little stroke on the neck, but then she had the nerve to shuffle her feet. The sweat dripped down my back even as the winter chill filled the barn. My teacher explained to me how the horse would be sensitive to my moves and that my legs and posture were very important in directing the animal. But it was soon apparent that my legs and posture could not be adjusted as long as I assumed the rigor mortis position in the saddle. After three lessons of the instructor's leading me around the circle, she encouraged me on with 'Well, everybody learns at their own pace, you know. Why, there's a man who started out just like you and now he's riding all over

England, blah blah.' She then decided to help me get to know my horse by grooming her. Nice horsie, pretty horsie. We did very well together until she broke wind as I brushed her tail. A normal person would probably have chuckled and figured that it was a sign of affection. I left.

Okay. I might be exaggerating just a little as I render the above accounts, but I'm not embellishing when I say that, out of all the places I have lived, England feels most like home to me. Underneath my sophisticated city girl veneer, I'm a simple country lass who has found her true destiny in the Rose of the Shires, as long as I don't have to get dirty in the process or see any snakes. And I actually like the grey skies; they keep me cool.

But now I'm going to get serious on you.

The simpler, quieter life I've been privileged to experience in these last few years, surrounded by the love of new friends within the safe parameters of the 'village', has helped me to discover that it is my nature to tell stories. Not just a hobby, not just a profession, but a genuine vocation. Out of all the gifts I have received during my stay here, the courage to emerge as a storyteller is the most precious. I can accept today that God, as I understand the Power of Creation, has given me a talent that has the extraordinary ability to bring to another person a smile, a laugh, a frown, a tear, a gasp, a nod of recognition, a bit of the relief we all need from the pains of growing up. And that this talent can be offered even with the imperfection of fat packaging, even when my fears of spreading cancer haunt my wee hours of the morning, and even as I fear my return to American suburbia.

Some of the best stories are true. I leave you with a memory of Scotland.

Gifts for the Storyteller

It is a cloudy, chilly, windy day this Friday morning in late November. As my friend, Michael, negotiates his car through Glasgow traffic, he admonishes me to remember that I am about to work with some of the poorest children in Glasgow, children who deserve the very best storytelling I have to offer. We approach the school, and I am reminded of the last visions I had of the South Bronx when I left New York in 1971 – urban decay and despair. Low-density council housing in various states of disrepair surround the school, while a monstrous industrial storage tank overshadows the playground. The streets are bare as most residents of this neighbourhood do not own cars. The school exterior looks drab and uninviting.

But inside, the atmosphere is electric with activity. As the acting head teacher shows me around, I feel the usual excitement that approaching Christmas holidays create in any UK school. I notice several artificial Christmas trees adorning the hallways. Little faces and bigger faces look up curiously as the big American lady passes by with her smiling hellos.

I work with several groups of children until playtime. The heavy cigarette smoke in the staff room drives me outside with my tea to visit with the children in the playground.

'Watch me jump!'

'See how I can do this yo-yo?'

'Do you know my Auntie in America?'

'Do that echo thing again with your voice.'

'Are you pregnant?' (No, just fat, I reply.)

During the next session with the infant children, I enjoy watching the rapture on the children's faces. My eye settles on one child who seems especially grateful for the story, nothing overt, just something in her dancing eyes. I get very emotional as I tell a Native American story about a boy looking for the wigwam of the Sun. The tears filling my eyes not only stem from the substance of this beautiful story, but from the gratitude I feel for being able to tell it. At the end of the hour I feel exhilarated and ready for lunch.

I am invited to sample the education authority's luncheon fare. I select a lasagne, some coleslaw and a few puffy potatoes shaped like smiley faces. I sit down with a group of children. A little blonde angel missing her two front teeth approaches me with a broad smile and a clenched fist thrust

under my nose. She tells me that I deserve some money for my stories, unclenches her fist and hands me three pence. I would no more decline such a gift than I would a lottery windfall, so I accept her coppers with thanks and return to my lunch as she wedges in next to me.

But I am unprepared for what is yet to come. The very little one with the dancing eyes that I had observed earlier leaves her table and, smiling sweetly, stands next to me with her hand also concealing some secret. 'I really liked your stories,' she shyly admits. 'I have something for you, too.' She opens up her hand to reveal a smiley-faced potato. I take it with reverence, pop it into the old cakehole and ask her incredulously 'How did you know I needed a smiley-faced potato?' With a grin from ear to ear she returns to her seat. When we meet on the playground after lunch, she puts her hand in mine. We stay fastened until the rain forces us inside and I am asked to join in the colouring-in going on in another classroom.

Life doesn't get much better than this.

June '00

Really Back in the USA

I feel like I'm living a double life.

In one life, I am going through the motions of repatriation – fixing up the house, getting the phone hooked up, the electricity flowing, the swimming pool rescued from a family of ducks and answering the frequently asked question 'How does it feel to be back?' with a generic 'Well, it's a bit difficult'.

In my secret life, I am paralysed by grief, retreat to the bed and cry buckets full of tears under the covers at the loss of England and the special life I had there. Then I lose myself in sushi or key lime pie. I watch my family so happy to be back in California and think there must be something wrong with me that I'm the only one feeling so dysfunctional. Even my little, afraid-of-her-own-shadow dog seems to be adjusting better than I am. My biggest fear is that I will not snap out of this sadness and will do something rash, like leave a farewell note explaining my need to find myself, desert my family and hop a plane to Heathrow.

But there's no doubt I'm back in the USA.

The ice cream aisle at my local supermarket has as many flavours and types of ice cream or frozen yoghurt as you have varieties of crisps. No fewer than five employees offered assistance as I roamed the aisles during my first shopping trip and left me with 'You have a good day, now' when their job was done. They all had straight white teeth, did not allow me to pack my own purchases, and my packer took my bundles out to the car. Abandoned shopping trolleys roamed wild in the car park wilderness.

I can hear the sound of crickets through my open window as I type on this balmy summer night. And the crickets, as well as the moths and mosquitoes, are still outside and not on my desk, because my window is screened, just like everyone else's in the neighbourhood (spelled 'neighborhood' here).

I passed by a Nation's Famous Hamburger Restaurant the other day. The famous burger consists of ¾ pounds of beef with all the fixings, a cholesterol nightmare needing four napkins to mop up the slop.

I saw this bumper sticker on the back of an old banger: 'I'll never tell where the bodies are buried.'

Membership in the local automobile club, including emergency roadside service at home or away, cost me only $40 (£25) for the year.

Yesterday, I got pulled over by a dishy motorcycle cop for doing 50 mph in a 35 mph zone. (This in a zone where the speed limit would have been 70 in England.) The fairies must have been on my shoulder, because I got off with a warning. I didn't even have to plead that cancer made me do it.

There are no three-wheeled cars in sight.

I've discovered that a local bookstore carries a variety of foreign newspapers. So I happily brought home the London *Sunday Times* last week for the bargain price of $8.00 (£5.00). It's good to know I can keep abreast of all the important events, such as Tony Blair alienating women, William's 18th birthday party and the antics of British football hooligans around the globe.

Old Mail editors have asked me to keep in touch with an occasional article, so you probably haven't heard the last from me. My tri-village claim to fame may be all I'll get. Besides, it keeps my lifeline to England open. Should your travels take you to the suburban outreaches outside of San Francisco, that porch light beckoning you from the highway will be mine as I would always wish to return the hospitality so freely given to me during my stay in the land of hedgerows and elderflower cordial.

Each night, as my head hits the pillow, I revel in images of England – grey skies, fish 'n chips, the Village Hall, Morris dancers, strawberry fields, kettles boiling, castles in the woods and smiling faces. Never do I want time to dim their memories, though past experience tells me it will. I painfully echo the Tin Man's words to Dorothy before she clicked her heels: 'Now I know I've got a heart, 'cause it's breaking.'

July/August '00